International Economics

© Himanshu Raninga

I: PURE TRADE THEORY AND GENERAL EQUILIBRIUM.

A- The exchange model and the gain from trade (assuming no production).

B- The production and exchange model and the gain from trade.

C- Playing with the models (role of growth, supply and demand shocks).

D- The Ricardian model (trying to predict the pattern of trade given the fact that countries have different technologies).

E- The specific factor model and income distribution (for instance: capital and labor for clothing, land and labor for food).

F- The Heckscher-Ohlin model (also called 2x2x2) (including the Stolper - Samuelson theorem, the Rybczynski theorem and the factor prices equalization results).

G- Tariffs and other recent aspects of protection theory, including some notions on public choice for international trade.

I: PURE TRADE THEORY AND GENERAL EQUILIBRIUM:

A: THE EXCHANGE MODEL AND THE GAIN FROM TRADE:

International economics is a field of growing importance because the world is more and more open. One way to measure the degree of openness of a country is:

$$\frac{Exports + Imports}{2 \times GNP}$$

Some countries are still very closed (Albania, Burma, ...). While, in the past, some countries tried to replace trade (Germany (before and) during the last war...). However, today, benefits from trade are enjoyed --cf. "breakfast theory".

If trade theory is the study of exchange, why is it a specialized field? In other words, why do we need specific models for international trade? Why can't we simply use standard microeconomics? (i.e. compare 2 countries as 2 consumers...)

In fact --because of nationalism-- we have trade policies (cf. Canada).

- factors of production are not mobile between countries (we relax this assumption later in the course)

To understand **the source** of the gain from trade, let's make the following assumptions:

In each country, there is an endowment E in terms of food and clothing.

Here, we have only 2 goods because 2 dimensions:

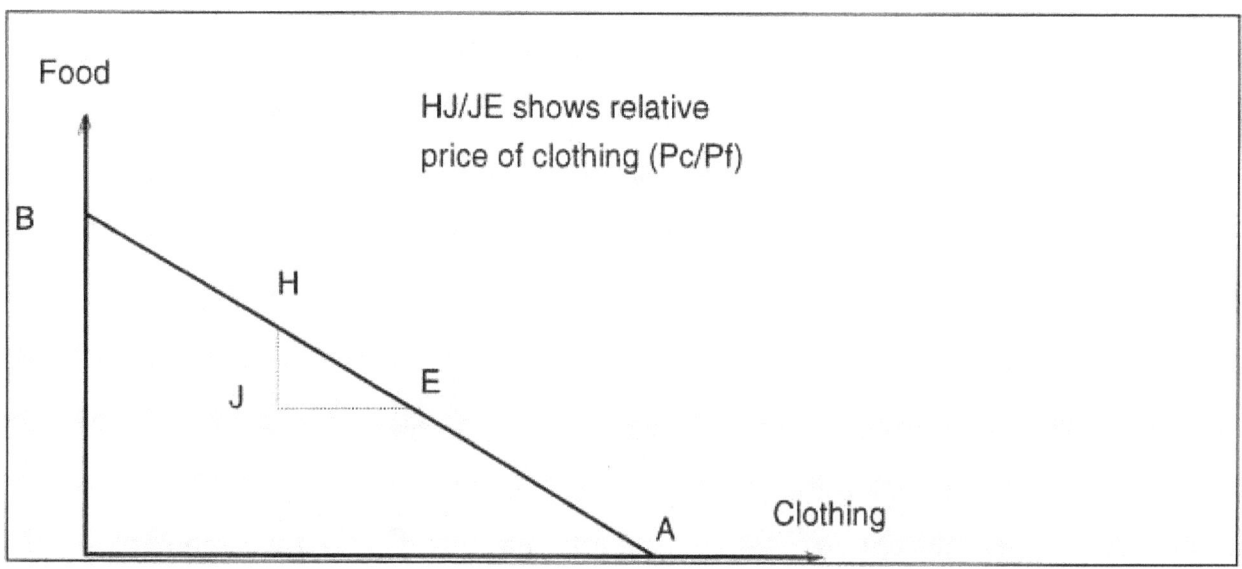

Any point on BA has the same market value as E. However, only E is attainable.

In the absence of trade --with other countries-- and in the absence of production, Endowment equals Consumption.

Now if the relative price of food rises, what happens: (hint: you still have the same endowment):

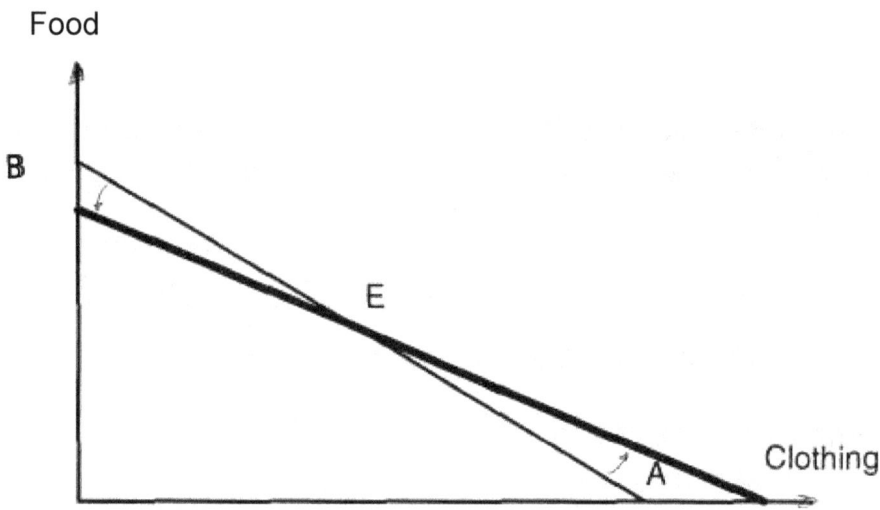

What is demanded by the consumer depends also on his indifference curves --and thus on his utility function:

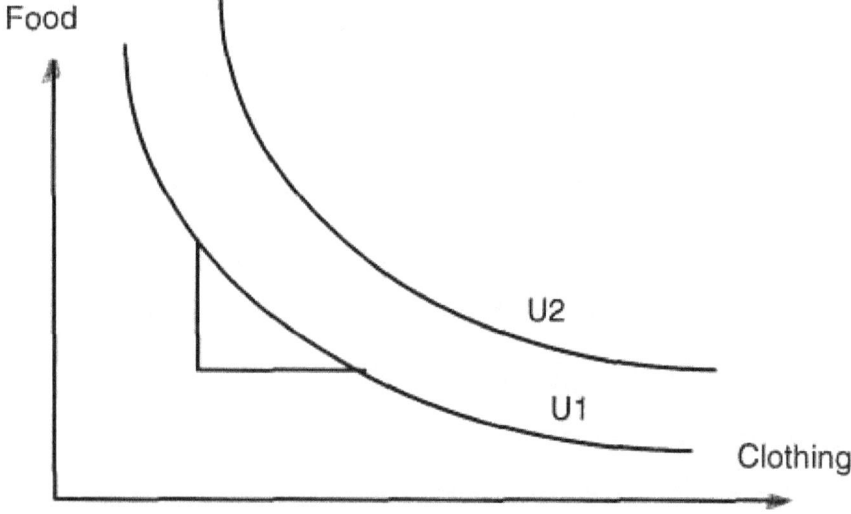

Note here: diminishing marginal rate of substitution is assumed.

For simplicity, assume that everybody in a country has the same utility function. We will briefly relax this assumption (to allow a model with **devo** and **repo,** but in general, each individual is assumed to have known and identical tastes...). **This is done to concentrate our analysis more on the effect of relative price changes.**

We can now derive the first key result in international trade theory. **Gain from trade arises when relative prices differ between countries in the absence of trade (autarky).** So when asked if a country could gain from trade, one should compare the relative prices at home, in autarky, (Pc/Pf) with the ones abroad (Pc*/Pf*):

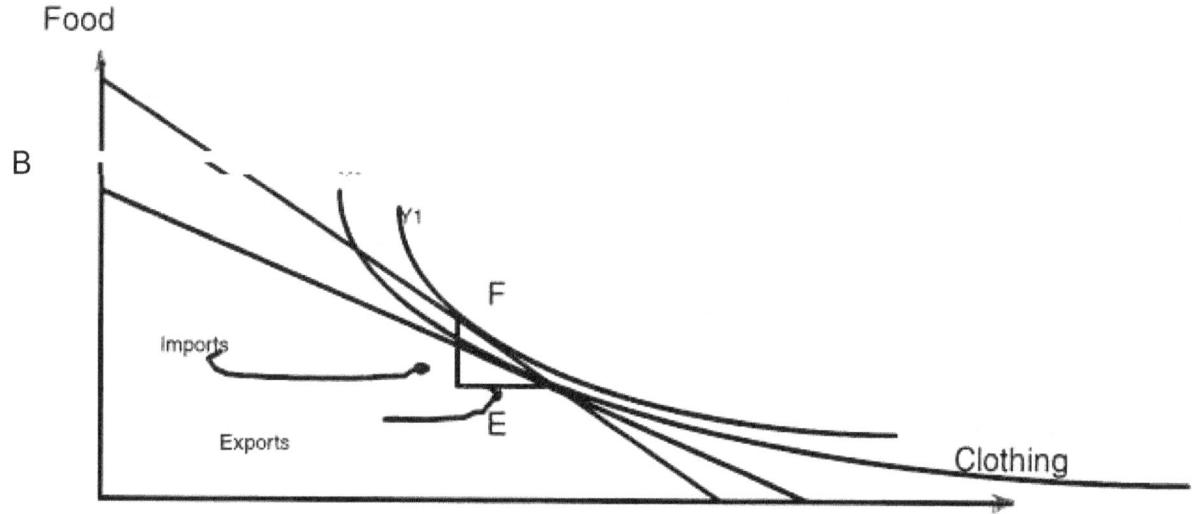

Gain from trade is the movement from Y0 to to Y1.

Here, we can see that the home country imports food and exports clothing. We can also see that there is balance trade, this is because the value, at international prices, of exports is equal to the value of imports.

It is also clear that, the gain from trade comes from the fact that you separate endowment from consumption.

Famous real life example: Prisoner of War Camp: everybody receives a fixed endowment of cigarettes, tea, coffee ... but taste differs so relative prices differ so there is a potential for gain from trade.

The constraints are:

$Pc.Dc + Pf.Df = Pc.Xc + Pf.Xf$ (at home)

$Pc^*.Dc^* + Pf^*.Df^* = Pc^*.Xc^* + Pf^*.Xf^*$ (abroad)

In our graph the home country imports food and exports clothing:

Value of export = value of imports

$$P_c \cdot (X_c - D_c) = P_f \cdot (D_f - X_f)$$

$$P_f^* \cdot (X_f^* - D_f^*) = P_c^* \cdot (D_c^* - X_c^*)$$

In order to find the relative price of food, divide both equations by the price of clothing:

$$P_c/P_c \cdot (X_c - D_c) = P_f/P_c \cdot (D_f - X_f) \text{ (at home)}$$

$$P_f^*/P_c^* \cdot (X_f^* - D_f^*) = P_c^*/P_c^* \cdot (D_c^* - X_c^*) \text{ (abroad)}$$

Now trade between the 2 countries will force the relative price of food to be the same: P

$$(X_c - D_c) = P \cdot (D_f - X_f)$$
$$P \cdot (X_f^* - D_f^*) = (D_c^* - D_c^*)$$

If these conditions are met (i.e. if the price P clears the markets), then we can say that:

$$D_f + D_f^* = X_f + X_f^*$$
$$D_c + D_c^* = X_c + X_c^*$$
DEMAND = SUPPLY

The balance of payment equilibrium condition is:

$$P \cdot (D_f - X_f) = (D_c^* - X_c^*)$$
the value of imports   =   the value of imports
by HOME   by the R. of the World

Graphically,

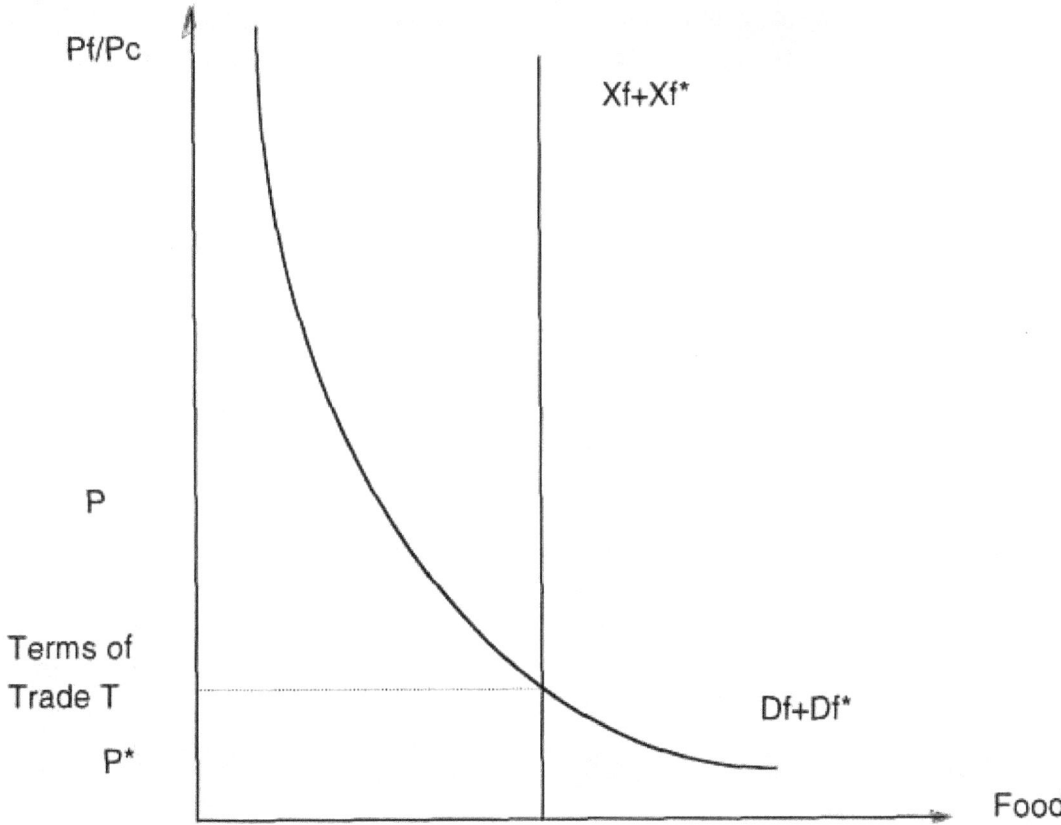

Or, alternatively,

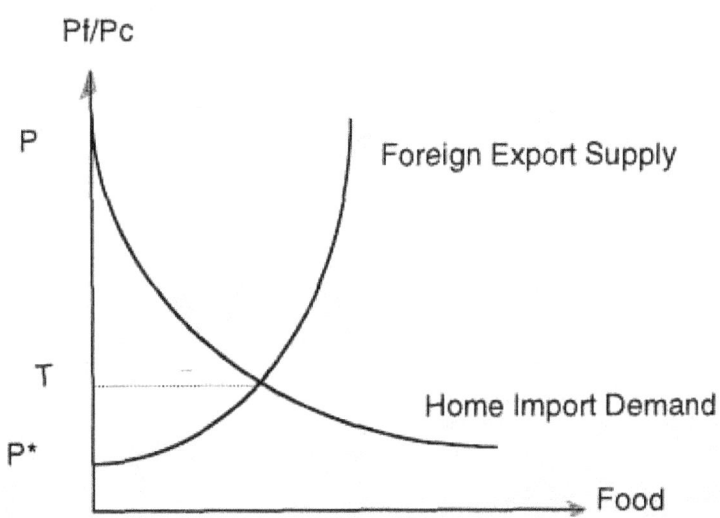

Product variety, taste and intra-industry trade:

When the European Common Market was formed in the 1950's, people thought that German wine and French cars would disappear and that Germany would specialize in cars and France in wine.

But in fact: Germany exports cars, wine, imports cars, wine and so does France.

Because people love variety (German wine is different from French wine, ...).

So we have to distinguish **gross trade flows** from **net trade flows.** These kind of models are called "intra-industry trade models".

Pareto optimum and Pareto Improvement:

Pareto improvement: a move from one economic distribution to another that leads to at least somebody better off and nobody worse off.

Pareto optimum: any situation from which a departure from would lead to a decrease in welfare for at least one participant.

This can be represented graphically by a Edgeworth box:

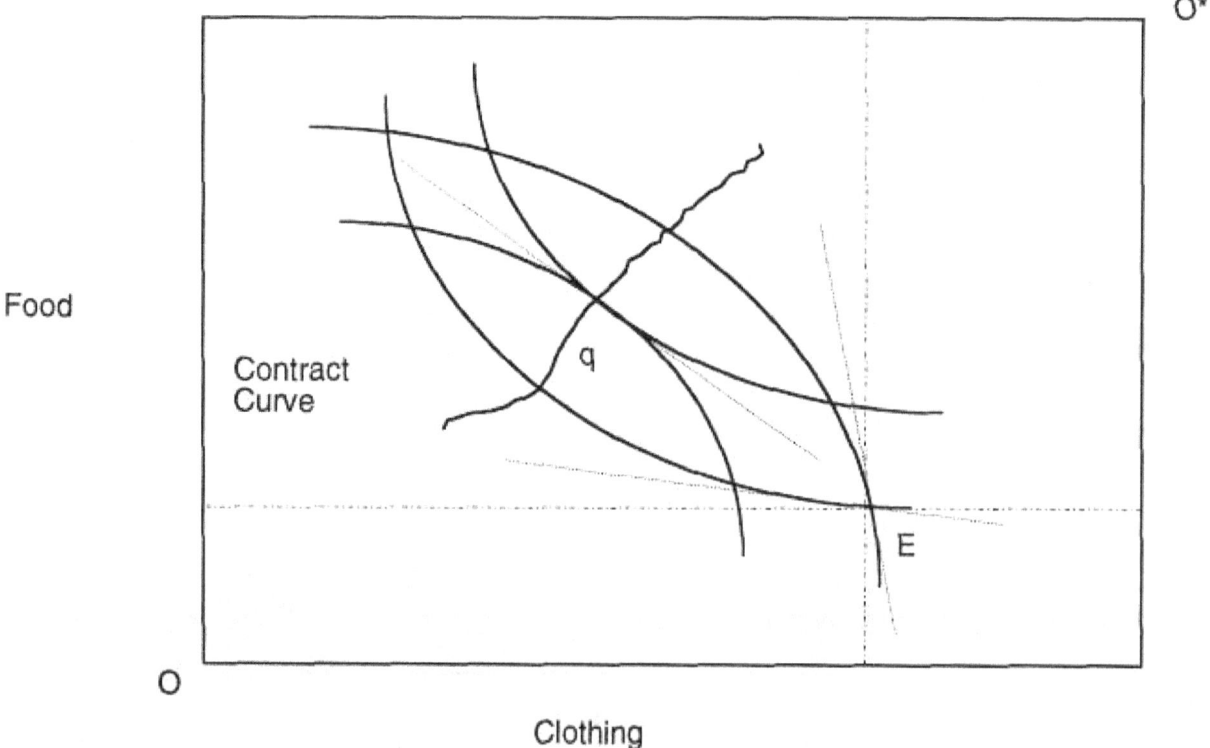

Losers of free trade:

Because not everybody is the same, some people might lose from free trade. Take the home country, it imports food.

Food

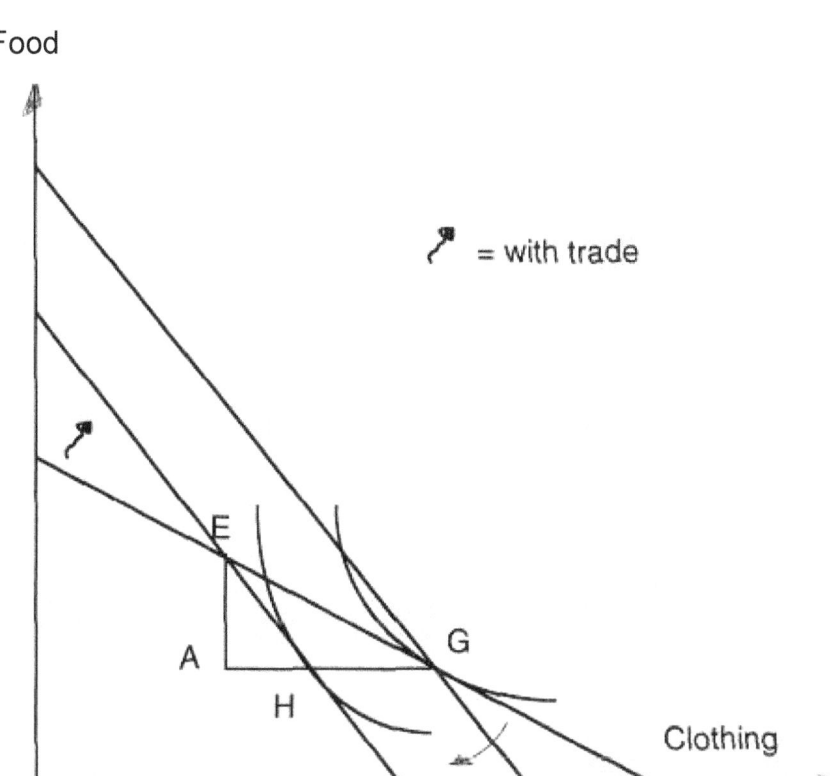

Comments: before trade, one individual (the DEVO) exchange EA of food to his fellow citizens (the REPO), receiving AG of clothing.
Compensating: if the person who was losing under free trade receive G as an endowment, he won't lose. However, other groups won't gain as much as before. So with compensation, G is the new starting point for the individual, then he goes into free trade.
Conclusion, even if some people could lose from the introduction of free trade, it is theoretically to compensate them.

Exercises:

1. "The worst a country can do by opening up to trade is to remain at the autarky level of utility" T F U?

    Use a diagram. Specify your assumptions.

2. What happens when the terms of trade increase? Use a diagram

Food

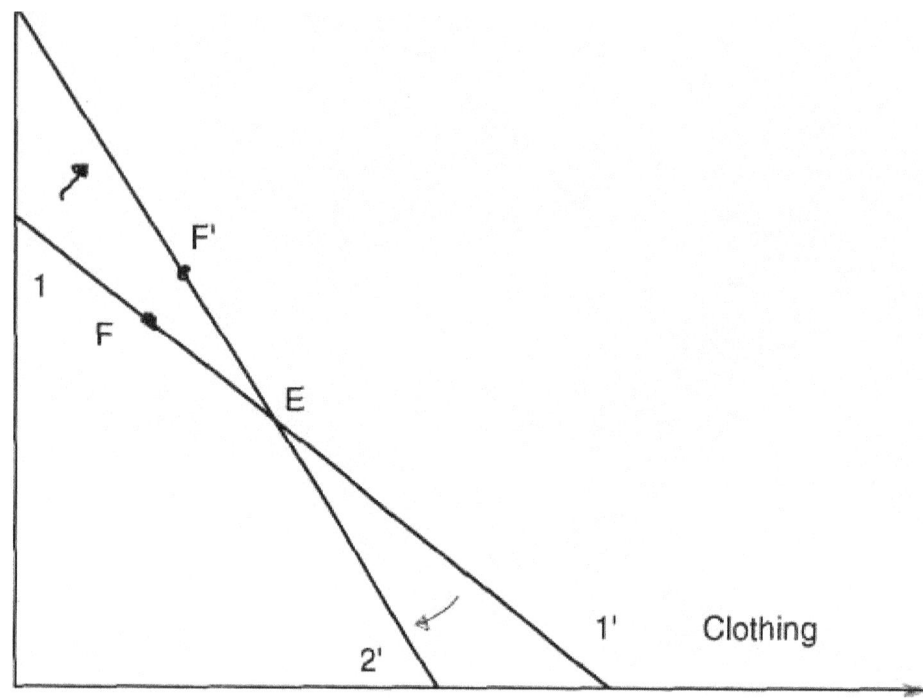

Comment: From 1 to 2, the relative price of food decreases, and thus the terms of trade improve (this country imports food).

Conclusion: an increase in terms of trade always raises level of Y, and reduces the level of Y*.

B: THE PRODUCTION AND EXCHANGE MODEL AND THE GAIN FROM TRADE:

In the first chapter, we saw that gain from trade without any production were taking place. Now introducing <u>production possibility schedule:</u>

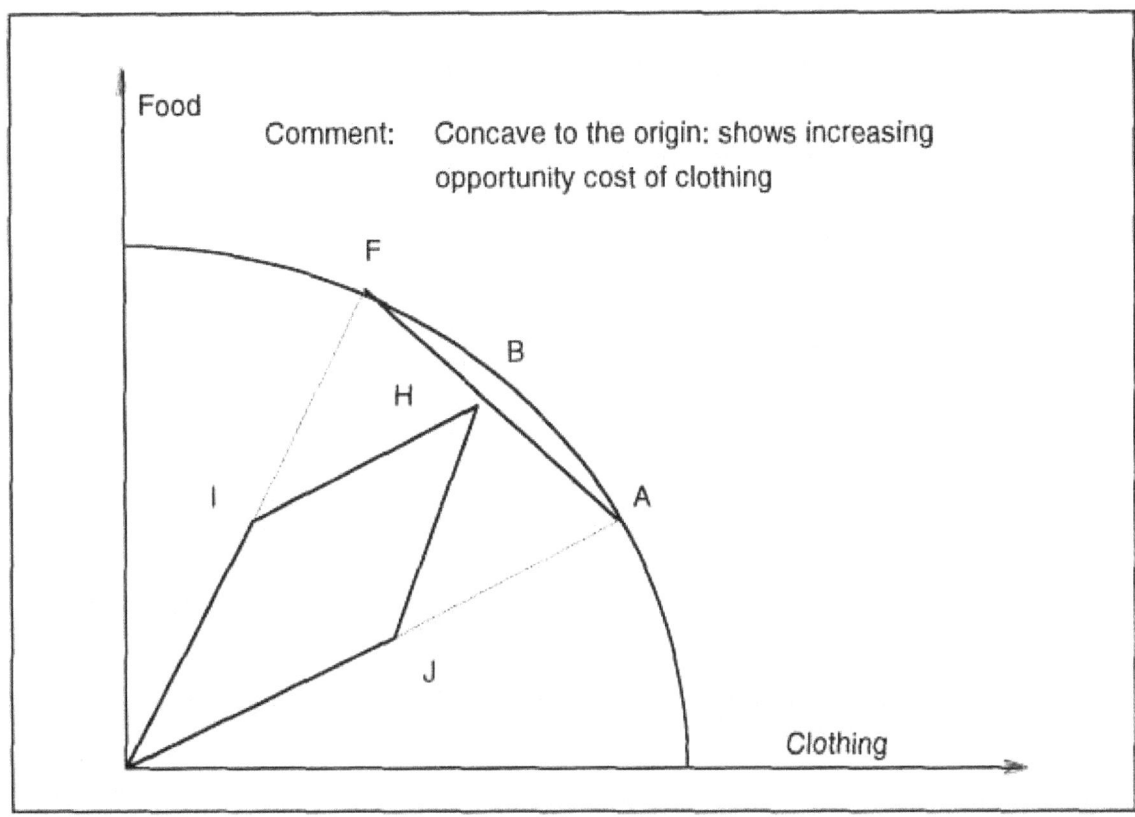

With CRTS, we have I (a certain bundle of food and clothing, produced using half of the resources) and J (same thing, role of CRTS) and I + J = H. But H is obtained by using 2 techniques, but one and only one is the best - so we can do better: B.

Thus we have shown that the concave shape was consistent with CRTS (more on that later).

In autarky, the country consumes what it produces, and so doing maximizes its utility, limited in that (i.e.: subject to) its production possibility frontier:

At point A, the slope of the line tangent to the PPF represents the cost of transforming an additional unit of food into clothing, this is Pc/Pf. This can also been interpreted as MUc/MUf.

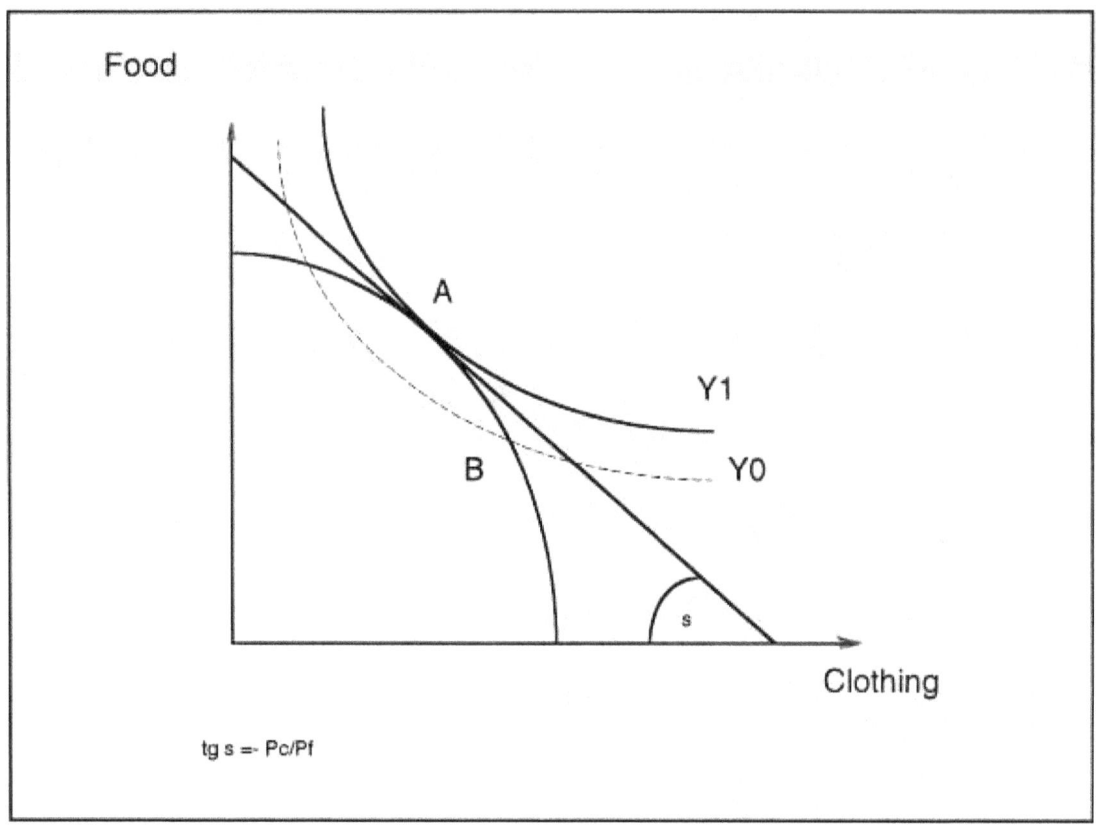

Now opening to trade, there will be a new relative world price different than the one in autarky. It will be determined by supply and demand in both countries.

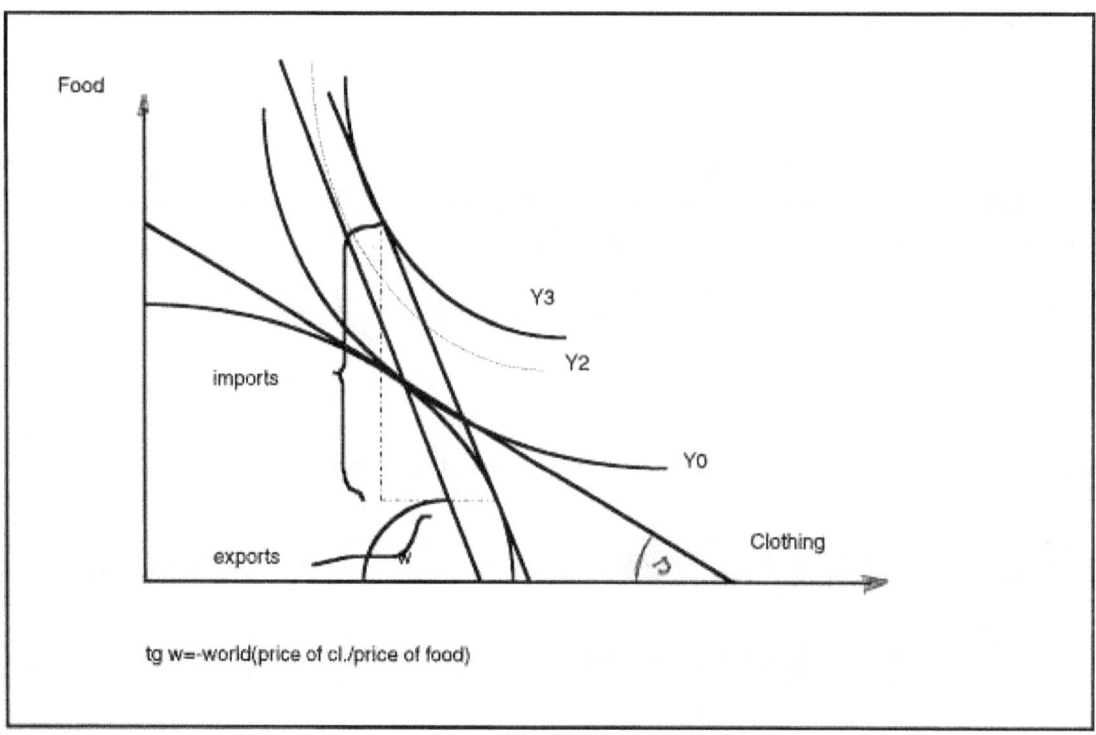

Introducing the notion of comparative advantage:

Here: the home country has a comparative advantage in producing clothing, because Pc/Pf is --in autarky-- smaller than Pc*/Pf*.

[and thus the foreign country has a comparative advantage in producing food]

This means that the home country has a LOWER RELATIVE AUTARKY PRICE FOR CLOTHING than the foreign country.

Trade Triangle for the Foreign Country:

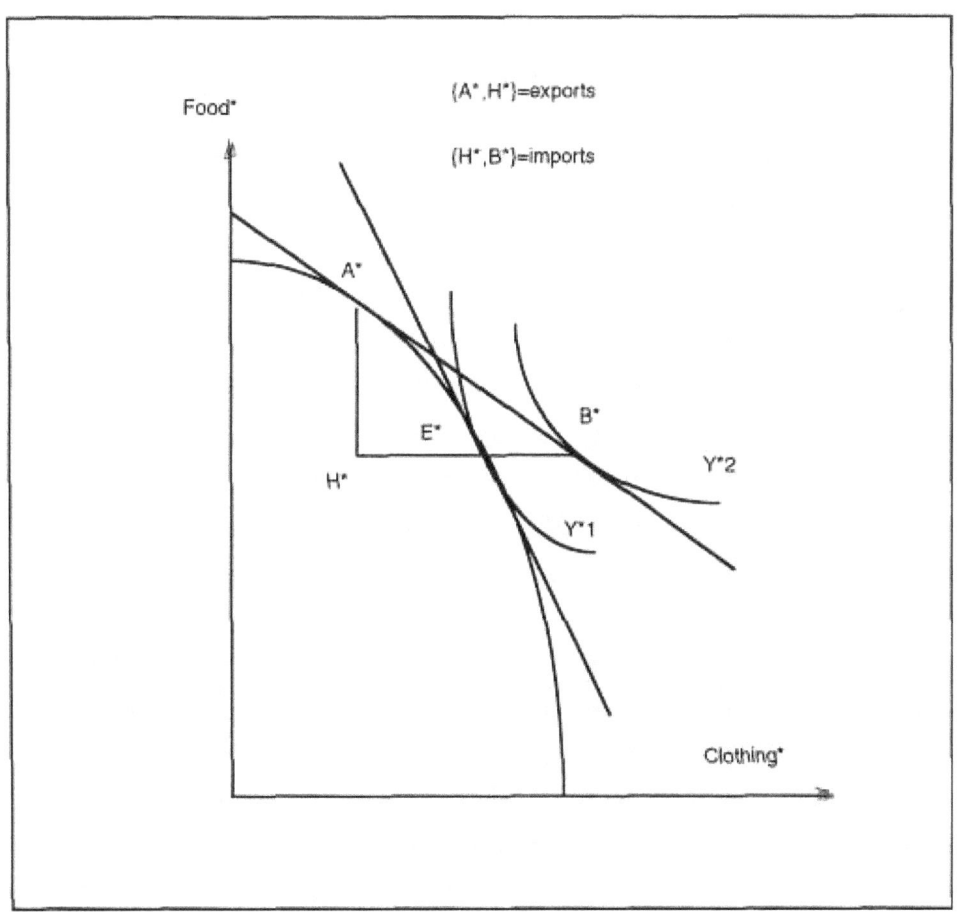

We can summarize all of this in one graph, by using the concept of relative supply curve and relative demand curve.

Suppose that the tastes are comparable, then comparative advantage and production bias are consistent with trade patterns. This means that the country with comparative advantage in clothing (here, the home country) will export clothing, while the country with comparative advantage in food will export food.

BEWARE: THIS RESULT RESTS ON THE ASSUMPTION THAT TASTES ARE COMPARABLE!!!

where T is the free trade price ratio.

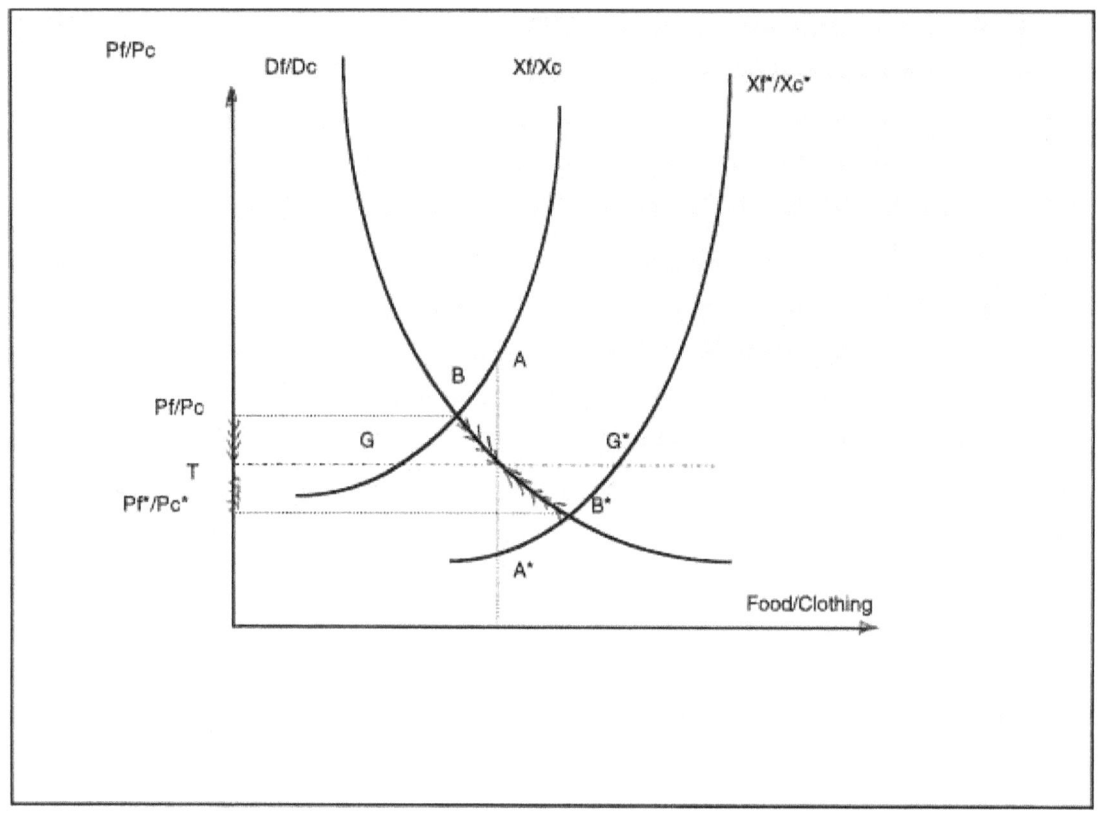

Why is that the home country has a comparative advantage (and thus a production bias) for clothing?

2 famous models will be presented later to specifically answer this question:

- one in which the technology of production differs among countries (cf. **RICARDO,** Chapter D of these notes)

- and one in which relative endowment of K, L differs among countries (cf. **HECKSCHER-OHLIN,** Chapter F of these notes).

Now, so far we have assumed that tastes were the same in both countries. So trade pattern was consistent with production bias (comparative advantage).

Now suppose tastes are biased. Suppose that the country that has a comparative advantage in food has also a taste biased in favor of food. (Similarly, the (home) country that has a production bias in favor of clothing has also a taste biased in favor of clothing.): when this occurs, it is possible that the country with comparative advantage in clothing imports clothing and the one with comparative advantage in food imports food!

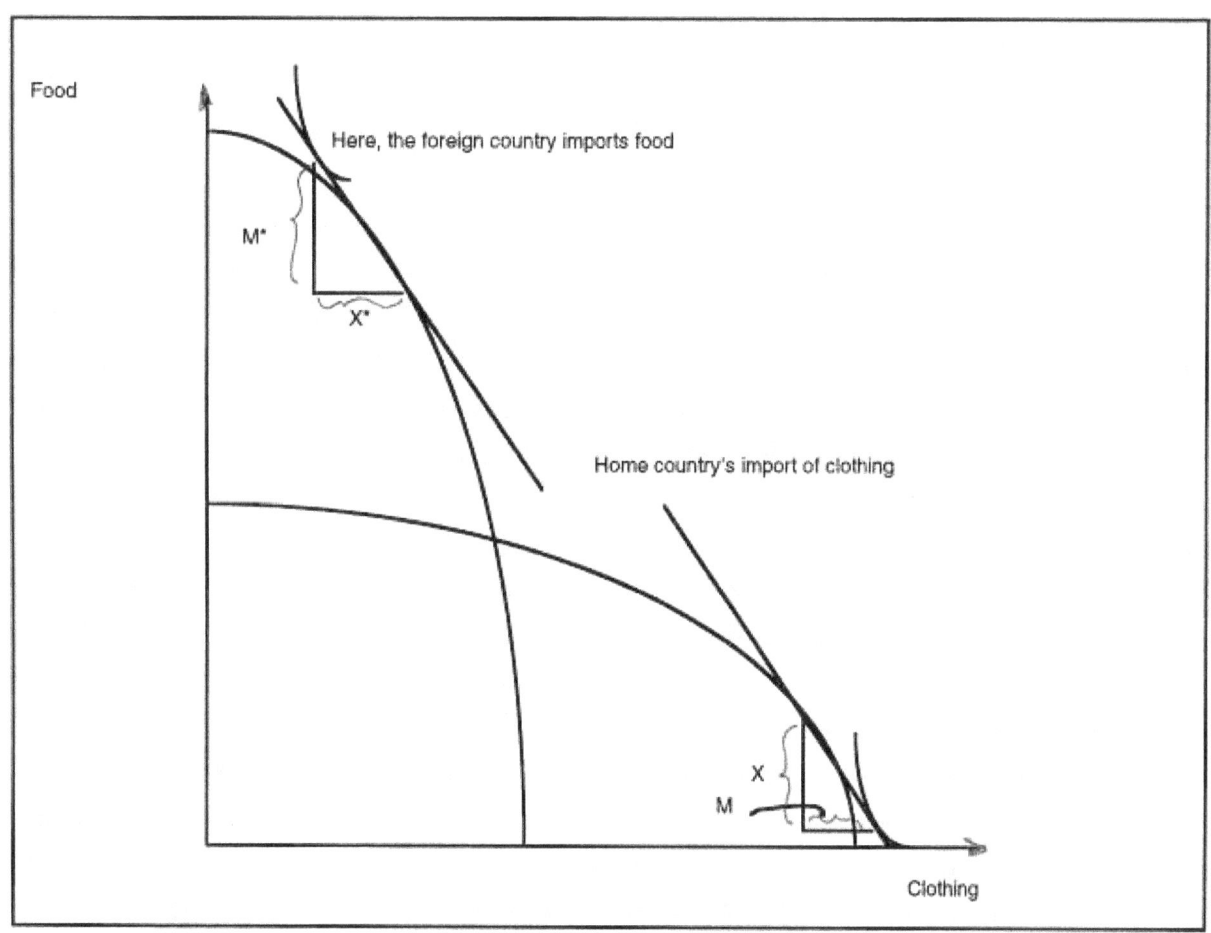

The role of scale economies and trade

If instead of producing 3 types of food (Fl, F2 and F3),

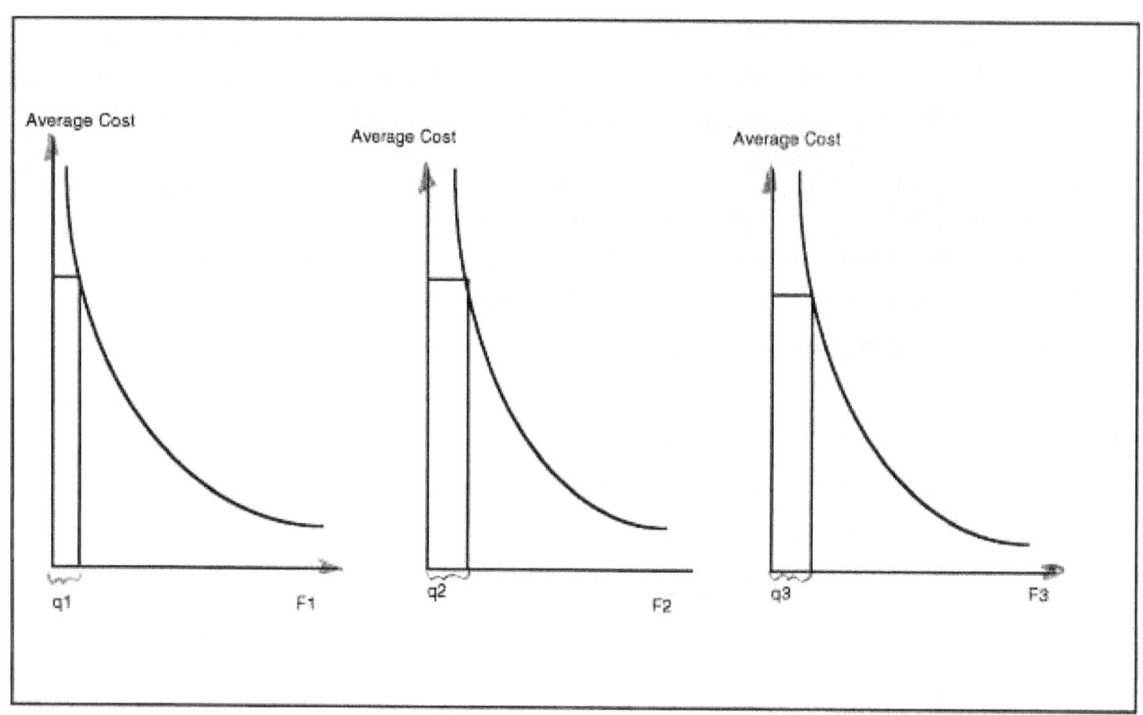

a country specializes in one kind of food and imported the 2 other ones?. What would happen? Because of the role of scale economies, this is decreasing average cost, there would be an outward shift of the PPF:

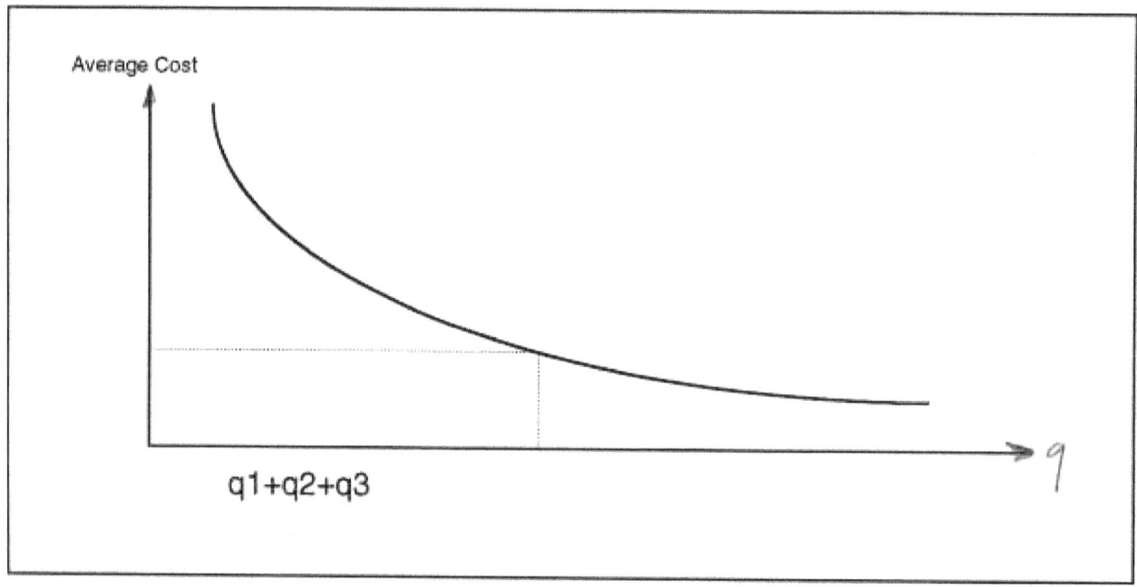

So trade, by allowing specialization, allows economies of scale:

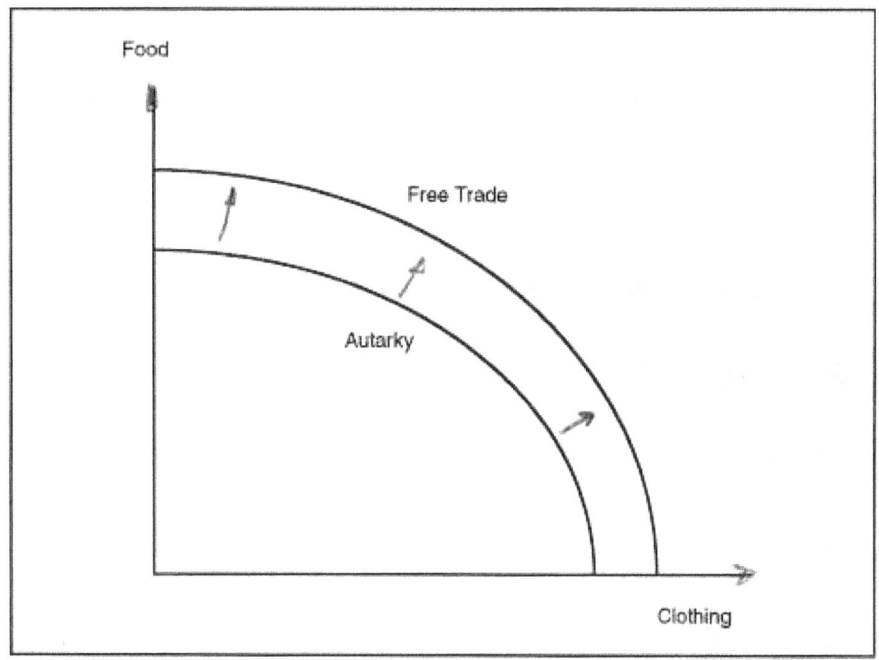

For example: wine: before trade between Germany and France, we have now ... more intra industry trade. Cars: France specializes in small cars, and Germany produces the large cars...

We can now summarize the gain from trade from the 3 sources

- from A to A': change in the relative price
- from A' to B': specialization (here in clothing)
- from B' to C': benefits from scale economies.

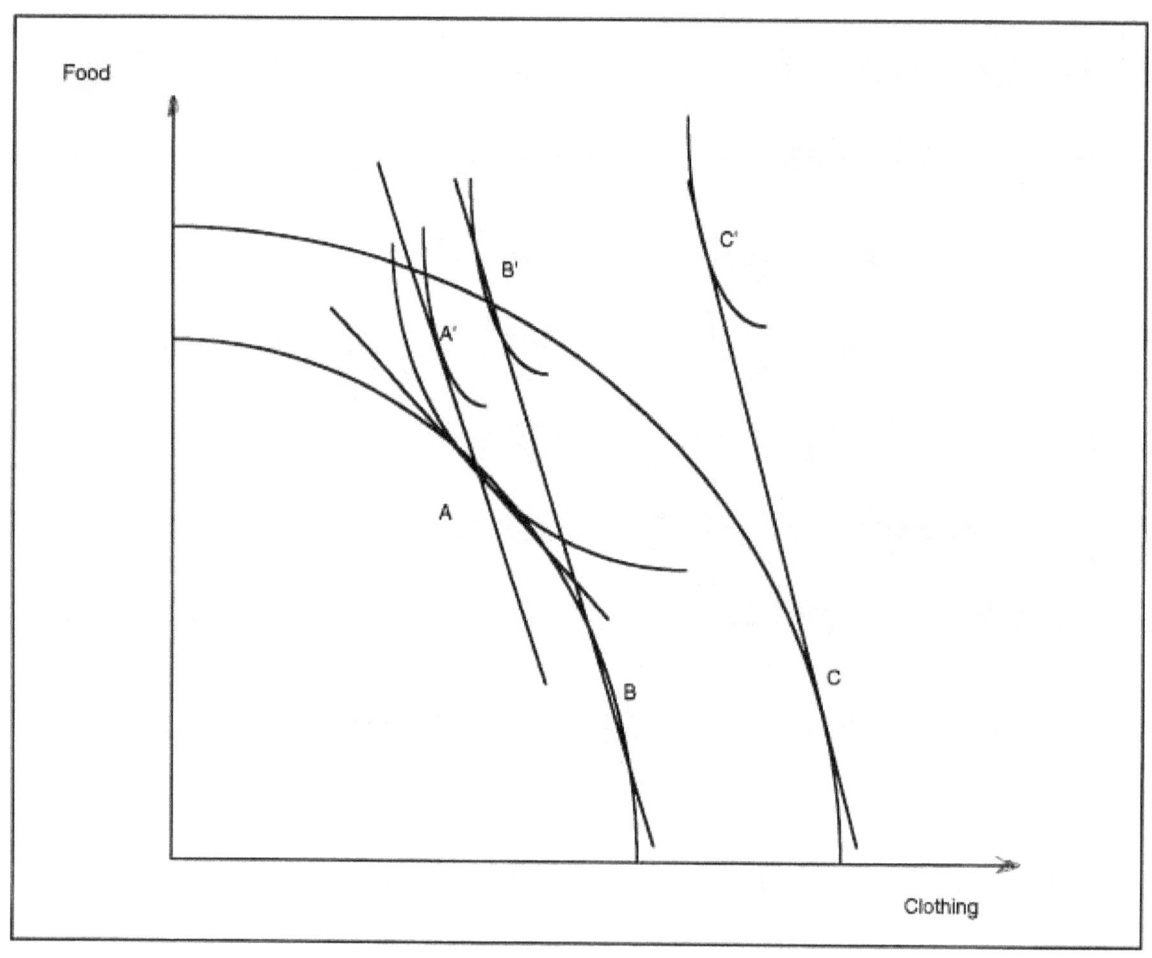

. Showing the changes in real income:

The aim of this section is to show that a change in utility is directly related to a change in real income:

Suppose we are in a two-commodity world,

$$U = U(D_c, D_f)$$ where U is an index of welfare.

Differentiating this equation gives us:

$$dU = \frac{\partial U}{\partial Dc} \cdot dDc + \frac{\partial U}{\partial Df} \cdot dDf$$

Dividing both sides of the equality by $\frac{\partial U}{\partial Dc}$,

$$\frac{dU}{\frac{\partial U}{\partial Dc}} = dDc + \frac{\frac{\partial U}{\partial Df}}{\frac{\partial U}{\partial Dc}} \cdot dDf$$

LHS > 0 if U increases, and we know that in equilibrium, $\frac{\frac{\partial U}{\partial Df}}{\frac{\partial U}{\partial Dc}} = MRS = Pf/Pc$.

What are the units?
CLOTHING!

Let's call the LHS = dY [measured in units of clothing], so we have -and this should make sense:

$$dY = dDc + P.dDf$$

But we also know that,

Dc + p.Df = Xc + p.Xf

Now, differentiating that equality leads to:

dDc + dP.Df + P.Df = dXc + dP.Xf + P.dXf

Subtracting dP.Df from both sides and noting that
dY = dDc + P.Df, we can simplify:

dY = dXc + dP.Xf - dP.Df + P.dXf, or if we simplify again:

$$\boxed{dY = -(Df - Xf).dP + (dXc + P.dXf)}$$

where: -(Df - Xf).dP is the terms-of-trade effect,
(dXc + P.dXf) is the (value of the) production effect

This equation means that a country can experience a change in income through either changes in terms of trade [ex.: if home country imports food, Df - Xf = Mf, as P goes up income falls as a proportion of Mt or changes in production or both (role of substitution).]

Substitution and income effect:

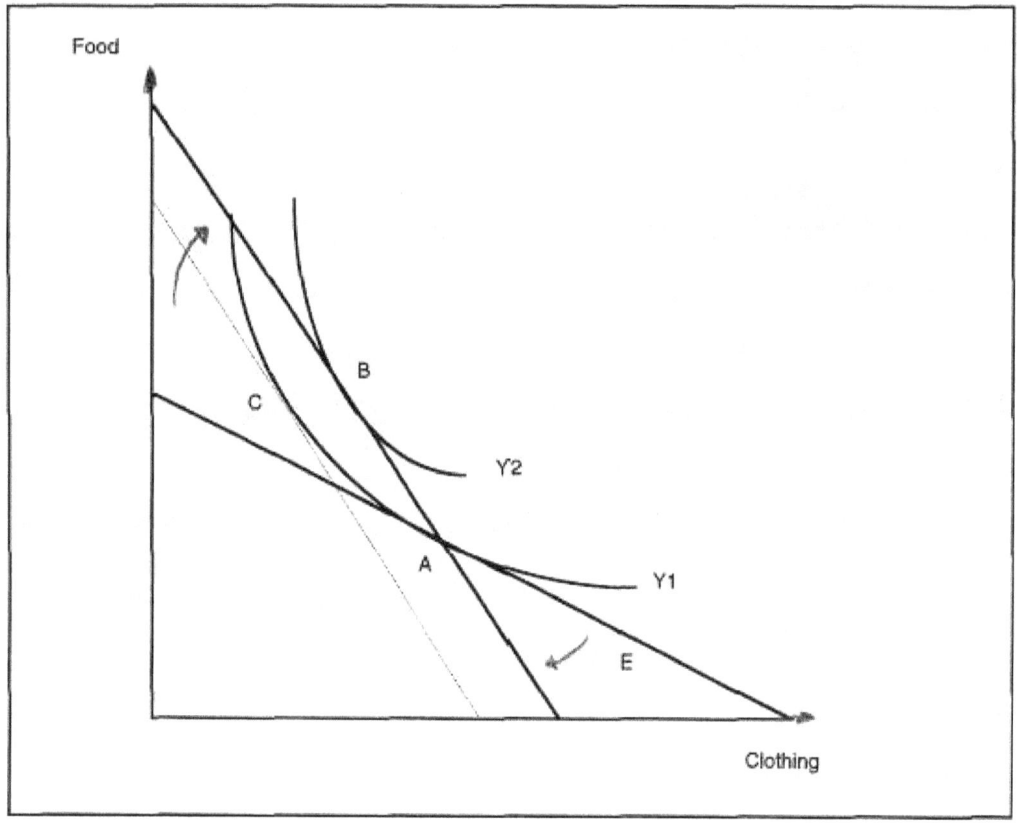

We start production at E, consumption at A -and the associate level of income is Y1

But if relative price of food goes down

A -> C (along the indifference curve): substitution effect

C -> B (from curve Y1 to Y2): income effect

A -> B: total effect

The elasticity of demand for imports:

Question: Suppose the food import prices rise by 10%. By how much will the quantity imported be reduced?

A: If quantity imported decreases by more than 10% -> elastic
If quantity imported decreases by less than 10% -> inelastic

Question: Suppose oil is imported and clothing is exported, and that import demand is inelastic. If the price of oil increases, will more or less clothing be exported?

A: More... Why?

C: PLAYING WITH THE MODELS (ROLE OF GROWTH, SUPPLY AND DEMAND SHOCKS):

Case I: A rise in foreign demand:

What may happen if there is a rise in foreign demand for our product?

Basically, there are 2 cases

    one normal (A)
    one looking like a paradox (B)

Note: never say that you "found a paradox", because a paradox is something one doesn't understand!

Let's study the two case in turn:

case A:

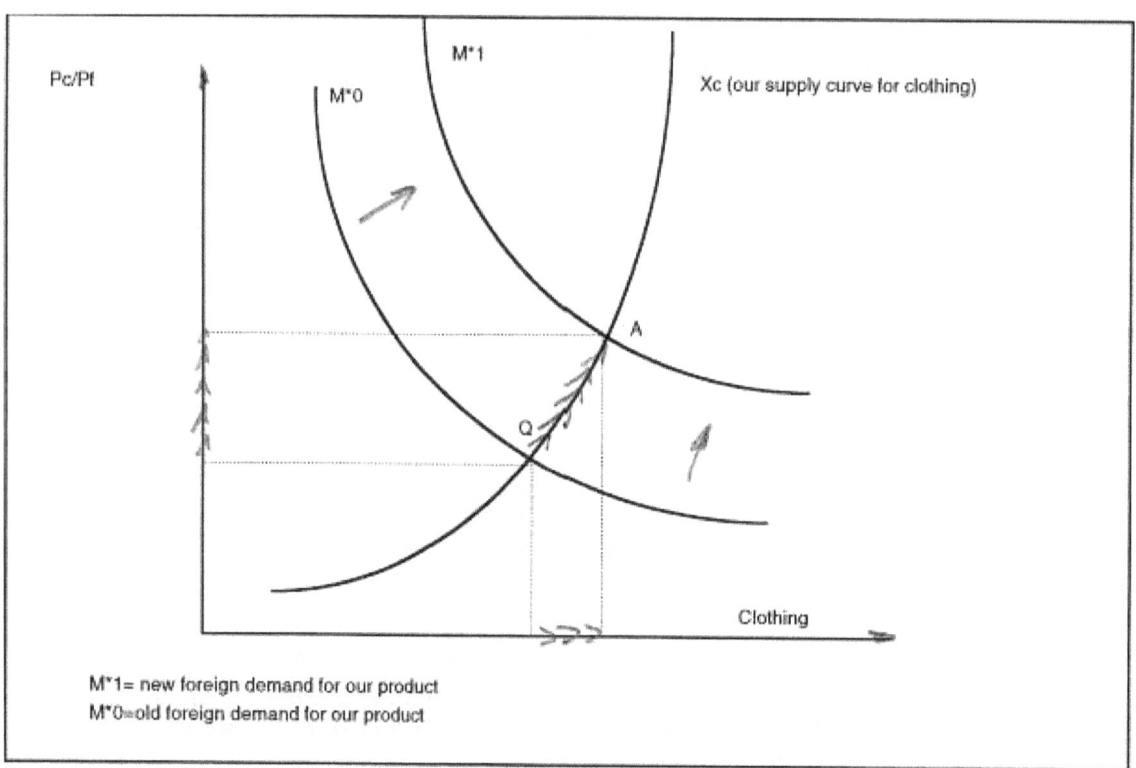

M*1 = new foreign demand for our product
M*0 = old foreign demand for our product

Comment: Relative price goes up and so does quantity exported.

case B:

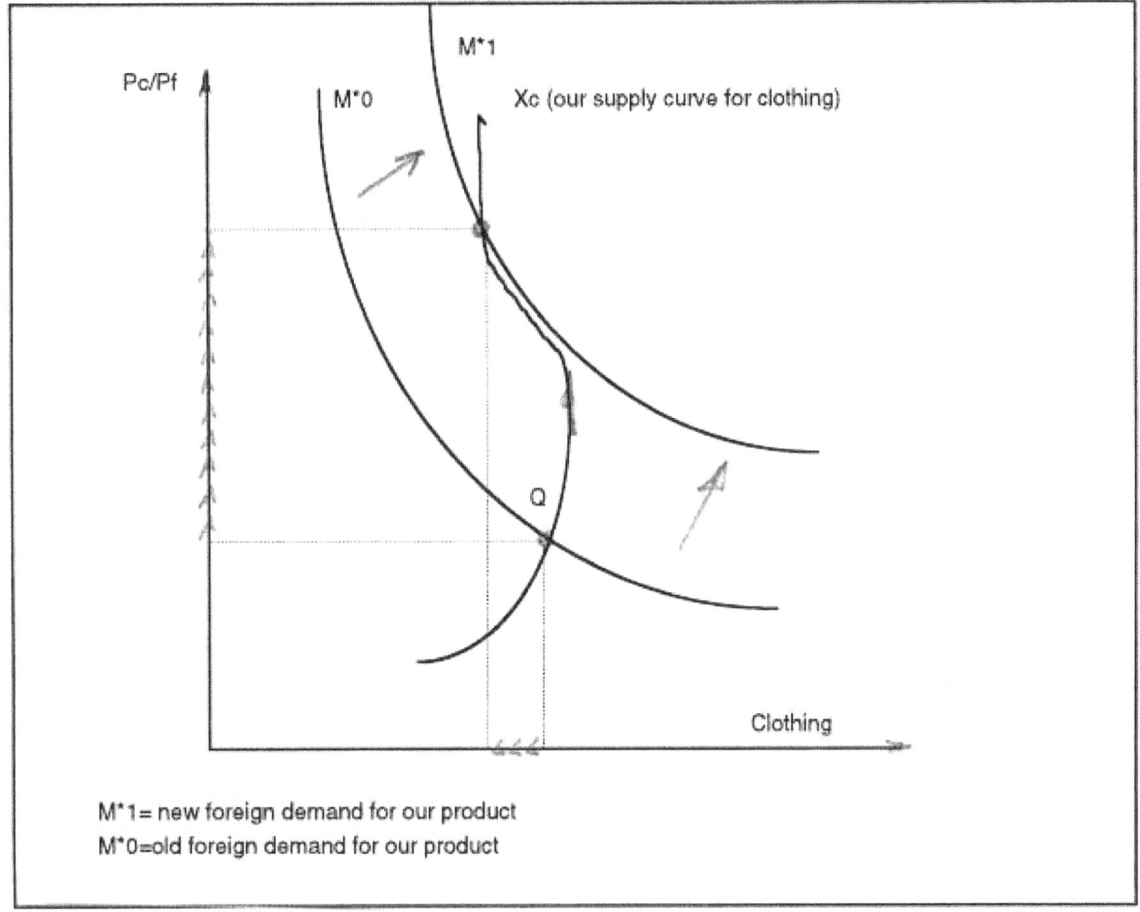

Why? Story: a rise in the price of exports make people richer, leading to an income effect (in addition to substitution effect). When income effect is greater than substitution -> exports decline).

Another paradox (!):

Reducing output of the exported good in order to increase the price and achieve higher level of income (cf. OPEC!)

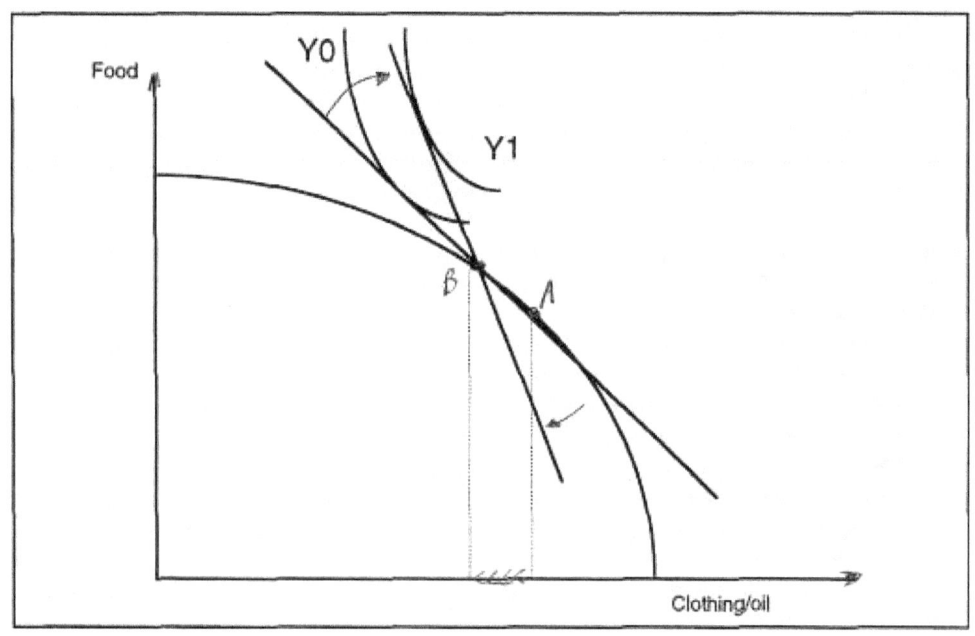

But there are problems with cartels (difference between a prisoner's dilemma and a super-game), leads to incentive to cheat.

Famous example of apparently successful cartel, diamonds.

What is growth? Expanding the PPF:

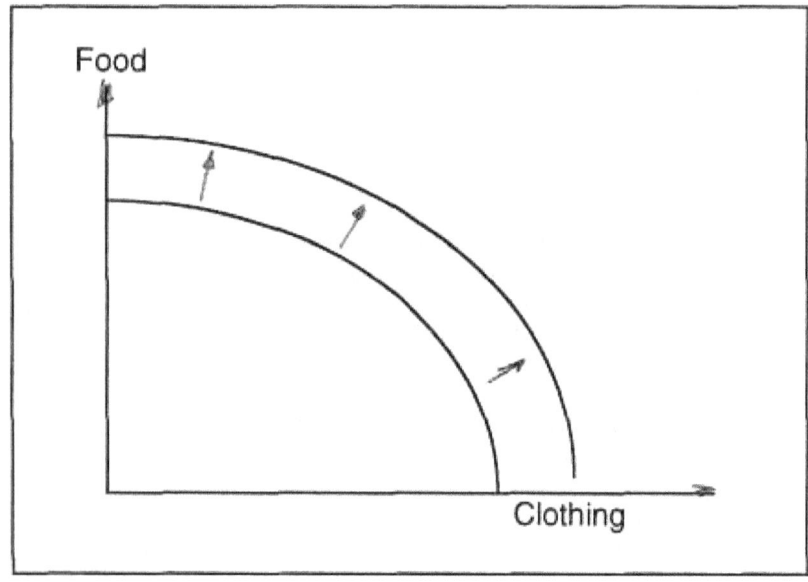

Now can growth hurt a country?
The answer is MAYBE!

This is the concept of "Immiserizing growth" (Paradox discovered by EDGEWORTH in 1894 and brought back in the limelight by J. N. BHAGWATI in 1958).

Story: growth biased toward the export, -> worsens the terms of trade...

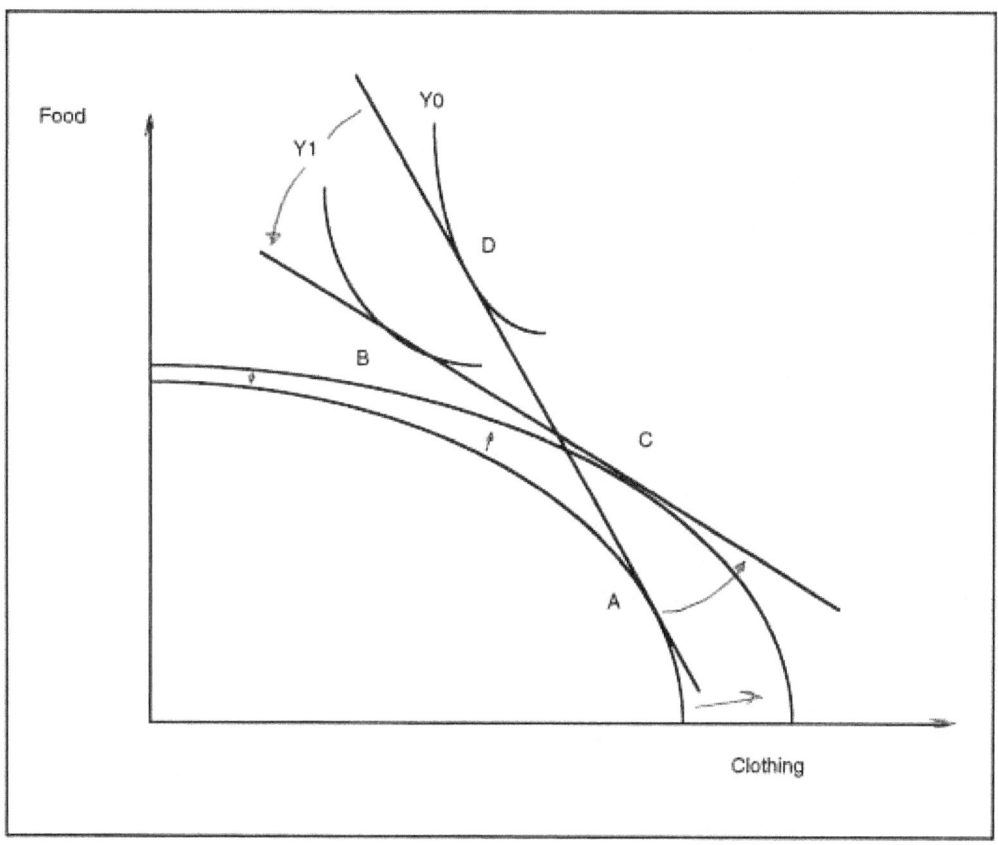

When does it happen?

There are at least two conditions to be met for that to happen:

Firstly, a country must be able to influence the world price for the commodity by increasing the supply...
-> generally a large country...
(cf. underdeveloped countries for raw materials)

Secondly, the demand elasticities for that good must be low throughout the world:

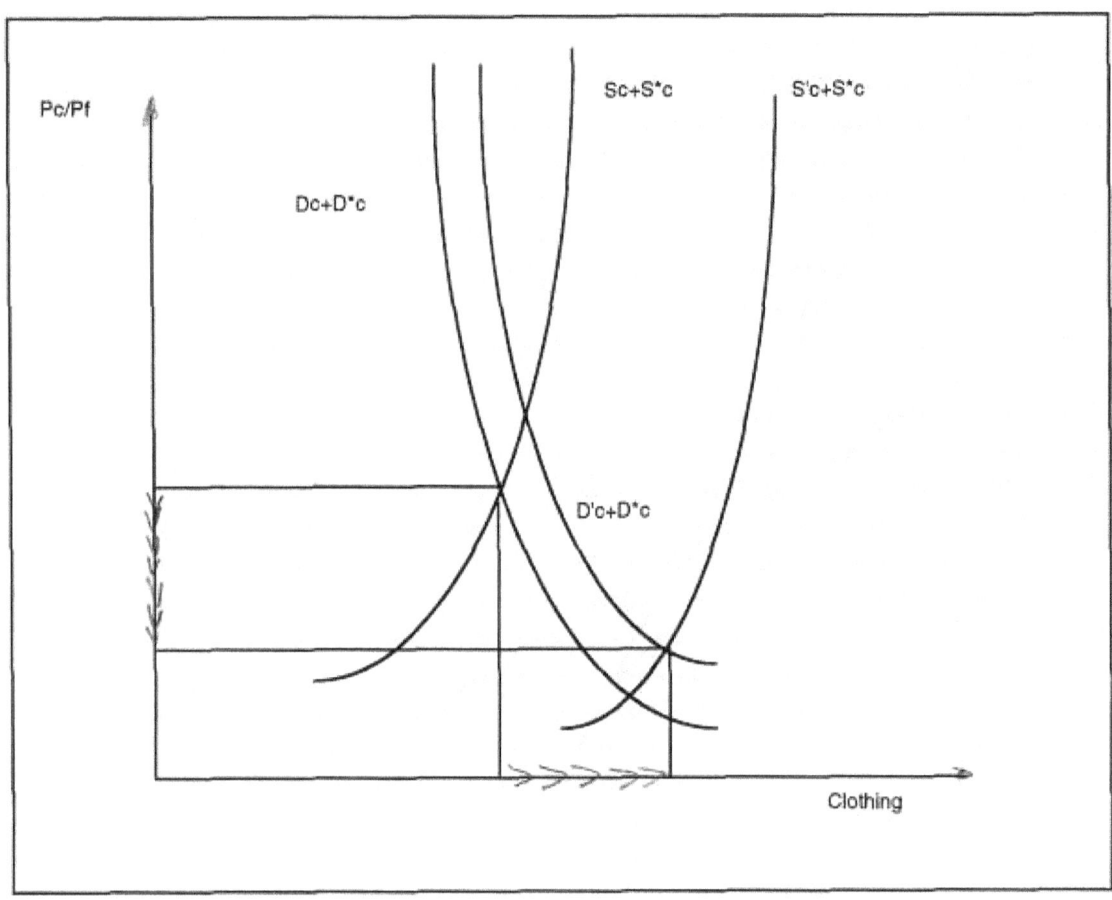

Does that mean that a balanced growth is without problems? The answer is maybe not!

There are two ways to see that (the second is linked with Immiserizing growth -cf. infra):

In the first case, the reasoning is the following:

> If growth is proportional at home, but there is no growth in other countries, demand for imports at home goes up so prices of imports will go up, but at the same time the supply for exports will go up too, depressing the price of exports: so what we have in fact, as the balanced growth starts is a pressure on the terms of trade, in other words, they can not stay unchanged:

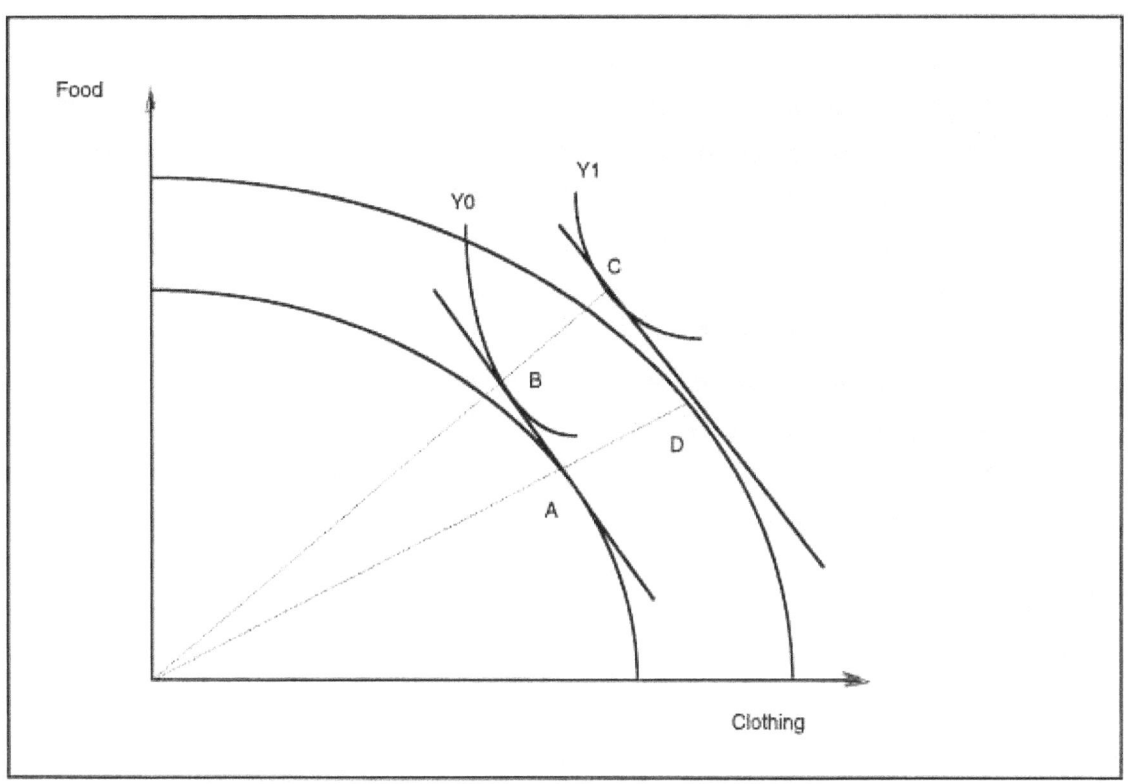

Comments:

||AB< CD|| This leads to pressures on the terms of trade to change

Famous case: France 1981/1983.

. MARSHALL LERNER conditions

When the sum of the two demand elasticities for imports (home country and foreign country), in absolute terms, is greater than unity, then a devaluation reduces the balance of trade deficit.

This is essentially a stability condition, as you increase the price of imports and decrease the price of exports, you reduce trade imbalance only if $e + e^* > 1$

Let's see that with a simple proof (In the second part of this course, we will see the graphical version of this condition).

P is relative price of food. (the good we import)

A devaluation is construed as an increase in P, so dP should decrease $\{M - M^*/P\}$ and this would improve the trade balance.

where:

28

M = home country excess demand for food, imports measured in food.

M*/P = foreign country excess demand for clothing = M*. But we divide by P in order to measure that in food.

For an understanding of the units of M*/P, we have in fact:

[C]/[($/F)/($/C)] = F, so M*/P represents our exports measured in units of food.

So the stability condition can be rewritten as:

dM/dP < d(M*/P)/dP   (I)

Let us define the relative change in price as $\hat{P} = dP/P$ and $\hat{M} = dM/M$

Dividing both sides of Equation (I) by P,

(dM/dP)/P < ([dM*/P]/dP)/P or simply: $dM/\hat{P} < [dM*/P]/\hat{P}$

Now suppose we start at an equilibrium where M = M*/p (our imports = our exports) (actually, to be precise, the Marshall Lerner condition is valid only when we start from a situation of balanced trade. If not, the proof becomes more cumbersome), then dividing the LHS of Equation (II) by M, and the RHS by M*/P,

(dM/M)/$\hat{P}$ < [(dM*/P)/(M*/P)]/$\hat{P}$ (III)

Rewriting (III), using the "^" notation,

$\hat{M}/\hat{P} < \widehat{[M*/P]}/\hat{P} = (\hat{M}* - \hat{P})/\hat{P}$ (IV)

We know that, be definition,

   e = elasticity of home demand for imports = $-\hat{M}/\hat{P}$

   e* = elasticity of foreign demand for imports = $-\hat{M}*/\widehat{(1/P)}$

where (1/P) represents the relative change in the relative price of clothing.

Remember that $\widehat{(X/Y)} = \hat{X} - \hat{Y}$ (proof: look at ln's!)

Also, we know that $-\hat{M}*/\widehat{(1/P)} = \hat{M}/\hat{P}$
So rewriting Equation (IV), we have: -e < +e* - 1 or, 1 < e + e*   Q.E.D.

29

Immiserizing growth

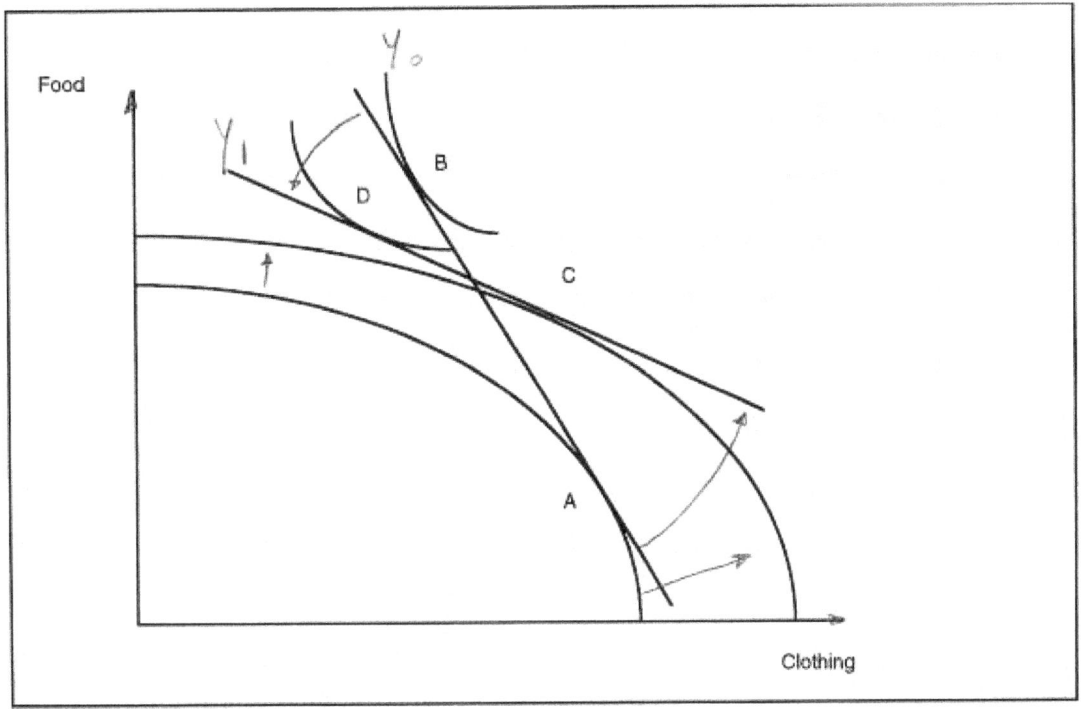

Here - as already seen - is a case of immiserizing growth: we consume at D after growth, which was concentrated in our expert sector.

. Now, with balanced growth could we be worse off?

The answer is perhaps: if the imports elasticities e and e* are very low... let's see:

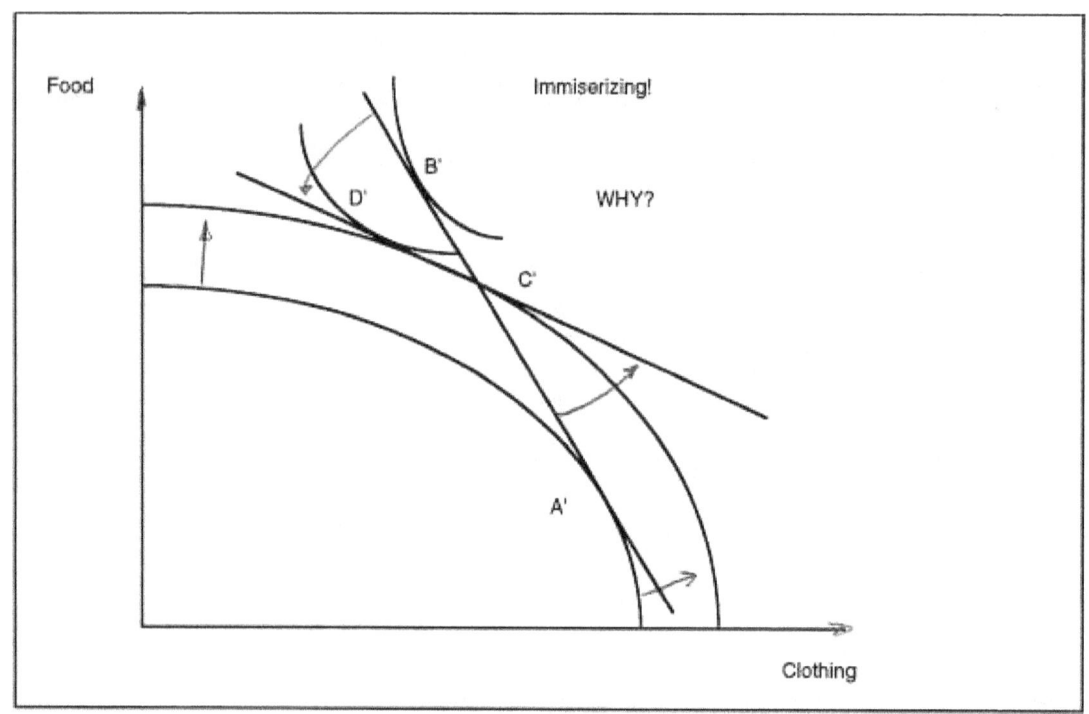

If foreign elasticity of demand for our export is low, as our (excess) supply increases, demand increases but by less than supply causing price to fall. But our imports are increasing (and because inelastic demands, Pf/Pc goes up ...).

So it is possible.

Growth in the import competing sector would result in an increase in our real income (actually here, inelasticity works in our favour).

As our import competing sector grows, we import less, this implies that the relative price of our imports goes down. And ... this might make us better off. This is illustrated by the following graph:

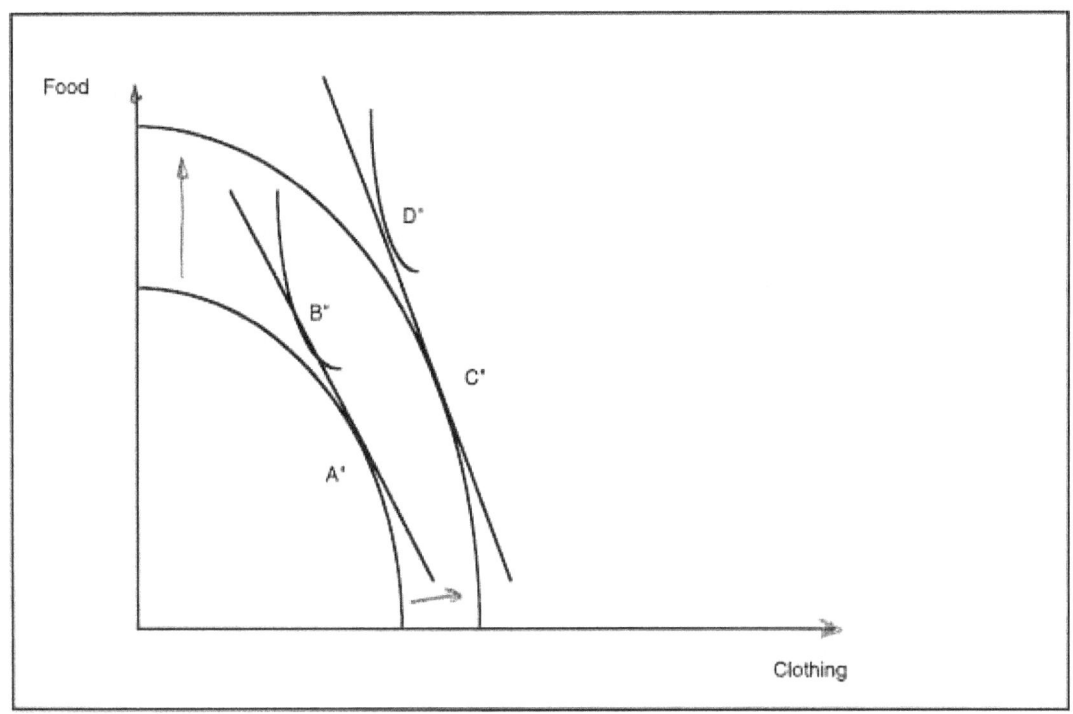

Remember: $dY = -(Df - Xf).dP + (dXc + P.dXf)$, $[dP=d(Pf/Pc)]$, here dP is negative, dXf is positive and dXc might also be positive.

Question 2 p. 68:

Q. If imports of food represent 20% of a country national income and the relative price of food increases by 10%. By approximately how much is national income reduced?

A. Food imports = .2 x Y
    Pf/Pc goes up by .1
    So, dy = -.2 (.1) = -.02 or a decrease in Y of 2%

It is a simplistic application of the equation:
    $dY = -(Df - Xf).dP + (dXc + P.dXf)$

Question 3

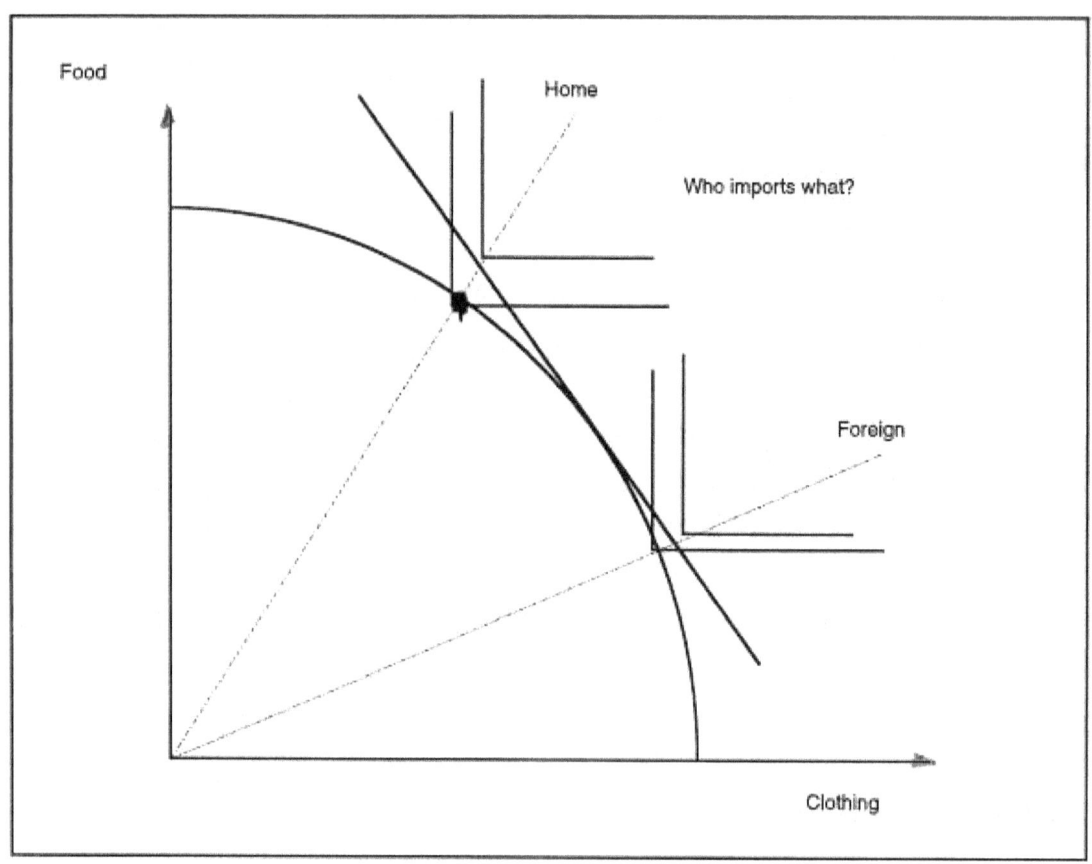

A. Home country imports food and export clothing.

D: THE RICARDIAN MODEL:

1817

Assumptions:

factors of production are trapped within the boundaries (of the country).

labour is the only factor of production that receives a return. Alternatively, we can say that the other factors are in infinite supply).

real cost/unit (average cost) is constant (so marginal cost = average cost). And our production function is thus forced to be constant return to scale.

labour pays the same wage in every occupation (i.e. within country, there is only one w.)

for simplicity, L and L* are fixed.

In a two commodity world, a country is completely defined by its technology.

Home: $a(lf)$ = number of labour-hours needed to produce 1 unit of food at home.

$a(lc)$ = number of labour-hours needed to produce 1 unit of clothing at home

Foreign country: $a^*(lf)$ and $a^*(lc)$

Now in each country, we have supply of labour = demand for labour:

$a(lc).Xc + a(lf).Xf = L$
$a^*(lc).X^*c + a^*(lf).X^*f = L^*$

And we KNOW - by assumption - that

$a(lf)$, $a(lc)$, $a^*(lf)$ and $a^*(lc)$, these technical coefficients are constant. Moreover, assuming, perfect competition (profit = 0)

$a(lf).W = Pf$ and $a(lc).W = Pc$ or $a(lc)/a(lf) = Pc/Pf$

Note: **$1/a(lf)$** = labour productivity = number of unit of food produced by 1 unit of labour.

We can now derive the Ricardian production possibility schedule:

NOTE ITS PECULIAR SHAPE!

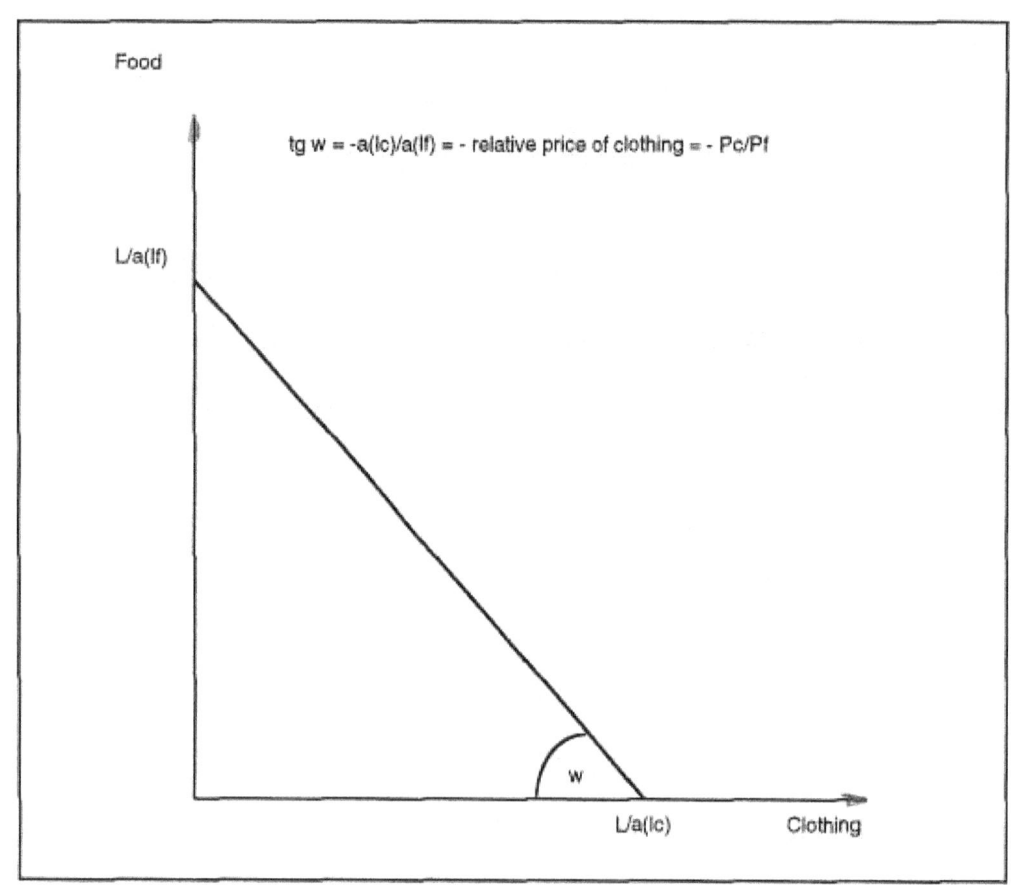

Before trade we have:

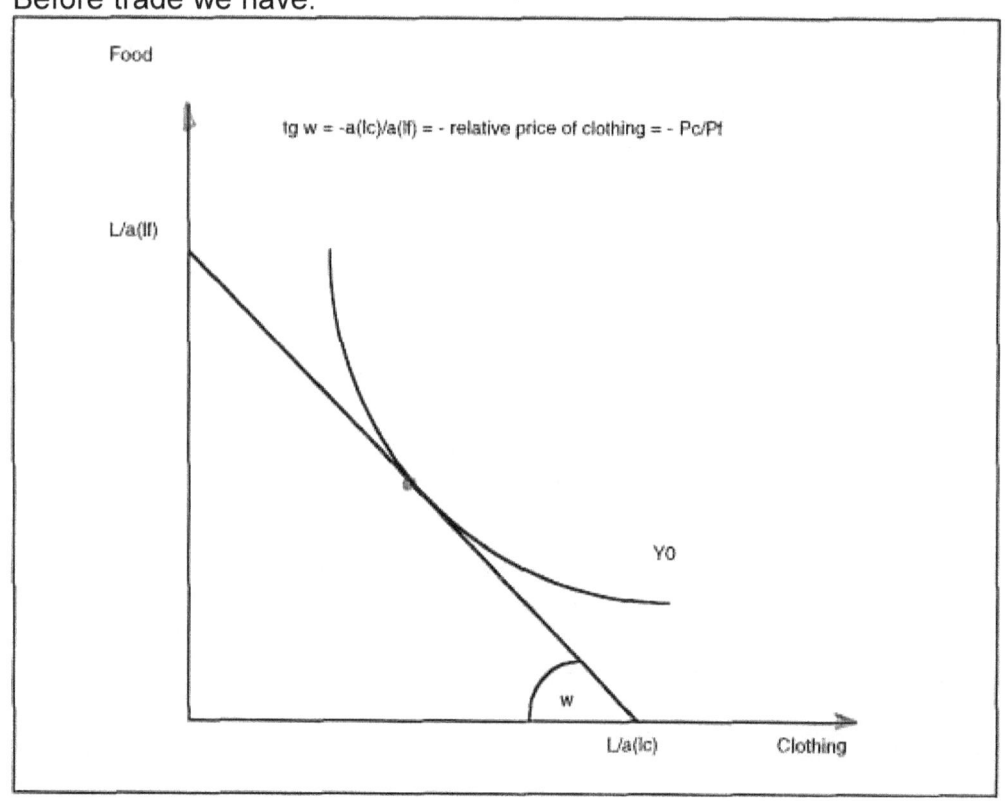

Note that the relative supply curve in a Ricardian world is horizontal:

a(lc).W = Pc

                Pc/Pf or Pf/Pc is a constant

a(lf).W = Pf

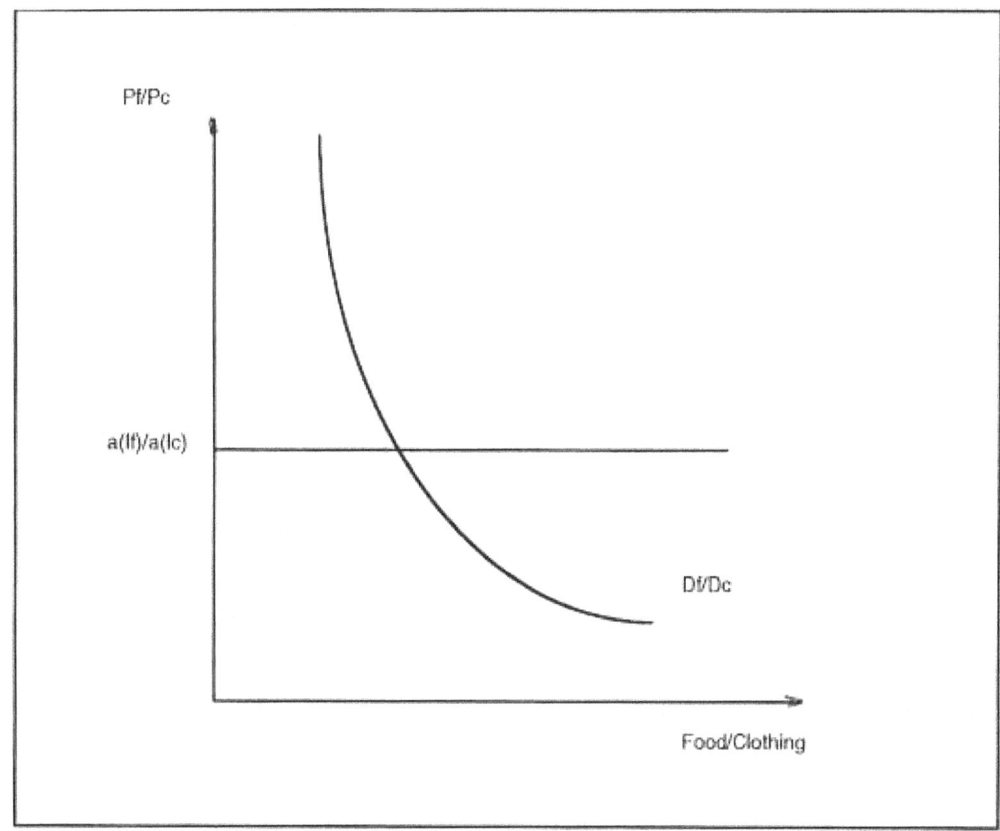

So (relative) demand has nothing to do in determining the relative price in a Ricardian model pre-trade.

Now, trade will occur between 2 countries if relative pre-trade prices differ. Remember, this is our usual criterion:

a*(lf)/a*(lc) < a(lf)/a(lc) and, again, here we will say that the foreign country has a comparative advantage in food and will therefore export food because his relative supply curve is lower.

So, in the Ricardian model trade pattern is solely determined by differences in relative costs.

Suppose, countries have more or less the same size and more or less the same tastes... then:

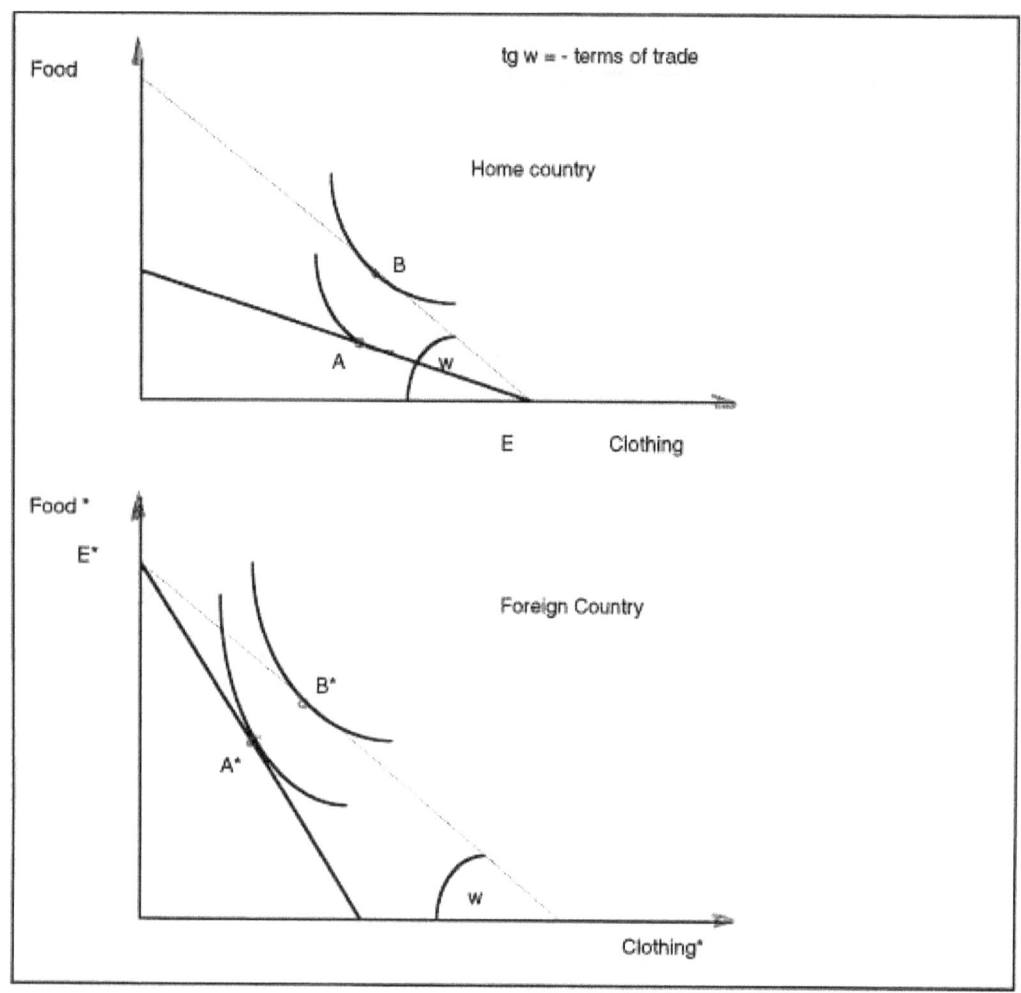

Note that, we have seen that, as a result of trade, in a Ricardian model, if countries are more or less the same size and same taste --see indifference curves in the above pictures-- this leads to specialization (this means that one country produces all the food while the other produces all the clothing consumed in the world. But suppose now that we have 2 countries: Huge - Small

Small has a comparative advantage in food and Huge has a comparative advantage in computer. Small will totally specialize in food. But Huge will produce some food and some computer.

We can represent the **world transformation schedule,** by adding up the home and foreign countries transformation schedule.

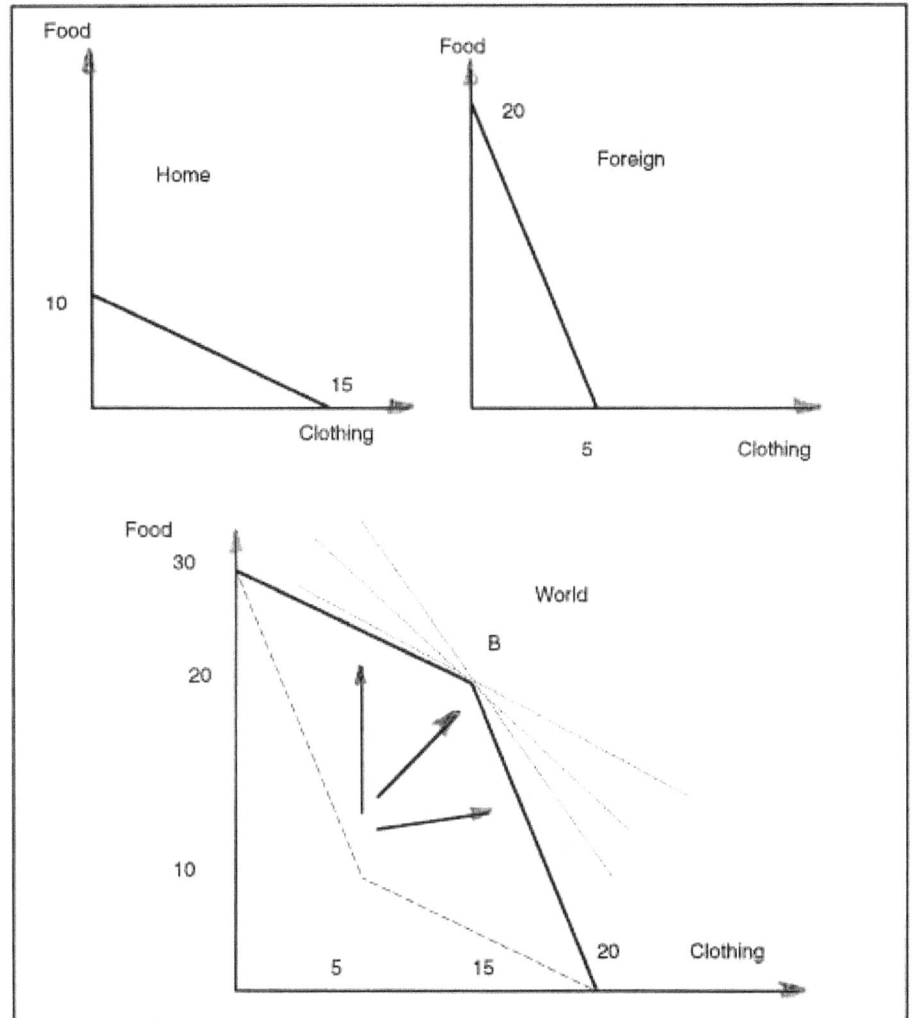

Comment: At B, each country is totally specialized in the good for which it has a comparative advantage.

World market for food:

Directly derived from the preceding graph.

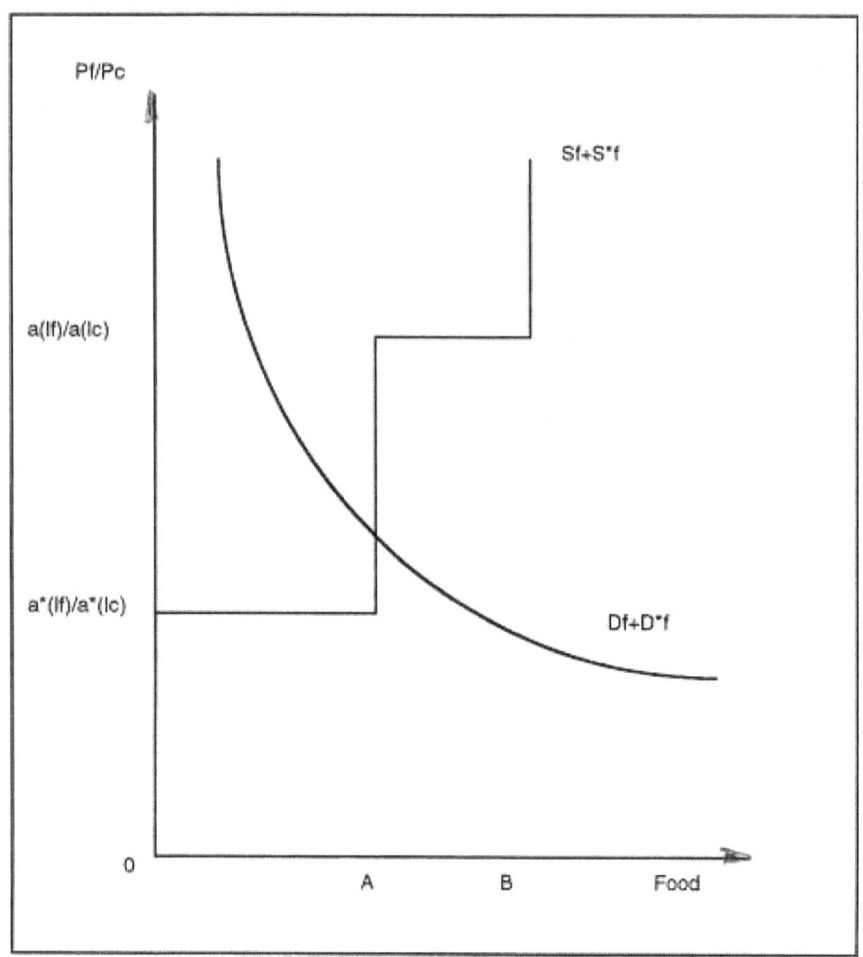

Where, OA = maximum amount of output of food in the foreign country, and AB = maximum amount of food that could be produced at home.

World demand curve for food: at each price, sum of the optimal quantity demanded in each country. (remember, **a demand is the result of a (constrained) maximizing behavior)**

What about wages!

Income distribution, real wage rates have been very important questions in pure trade theory. For instance, the free-trade debate in North America, is --in fact-- all about that.

Remember, we assume the Labour (the only factor of production) is trapped in each country. Labour does not cross borders. Remember, this is a Ricardian model dating from 1817. In general, in the models we will see, factors of production can move from industry to industry [unless they are called "specific factor" **as in our next chapter].**

Some terminology:

If competition exists, there is no profit, so:

Pc $a(lc).w + a(kc).r = a(lc).w$

Pf $a(lf).w + a(kf).r = a(lf).w$

Concerning the role of capital, there are two ways of seeing it: firstly, $a(kc) = a(kf) = 0$, or secondly, that the supply of capital is infinite so that $r = 0$.

Also, there is **only one** wage rate in a country. This is accomplished through competition mechanism. If, there are 2 wage rates, something is preventing competition from occurring. This has to be explained. In general, this would mean that we have two kinds of labor, L1 and L2, as two kind of factors of production.
But remember here, RICARDIAN model: - only one kind of labour. So only one wage rate.

Going back to our competitive conditions:

$a(lc).w$ Pc

$a(lf).w$ Pf

Now, what happens to one industry if $a(lc).w > Pc$?
Very simple (simplistic?) $Xc = 0$.

Note that this model, as well as the next ones are very Walrasian, in the sense, that there is no time dimension, all adjustments are instantaneous and drastic decisions are taken easily, for instance, total specialization in one industry, and there is never any factor of production that stays unemployed.

$a(lc).w = Pc$ so $w = Pc.(1/a(lc))$

where $(1/a(lc))$ is the labor productivity, or the marginal product or the average product. So w is the <u>value</u> of the labor productivity. So wage rate is linked to the commodity price and to physical productivity.

So when we compare w and w*, we must take into account:

      1)   **terms of trade**
      2)   **labour productivity in both countries.**

So, there is no reason why - if one uses this model - the wage rate should be identical in both countries.
Example:

Before trade, in a competitive solution:

$$\begin{cases} a(lc).w = Pc \\ a(lf).w = Pf \end{cases} \text{so } a(lc)/a(lf) = Pc/Pf$$

$$\begin{cases} a^*(lc).w^* = P^*c \\ a^*(lf).w^* = P^*f \end{cases} \text{so } a^*(lc)/a^*(lf) = P^*c/P^*f$$

Just like in the first chapters of these notes, let's suppose:

$a(lc)/a(lf) < a^*(lc)/a^*(lf)$

so $Pc/Pf < P^*c/P^*f$

We are in autarky. But, with free trade, suppose:

$Pc/Pf < P < P^*c/P^*f$

where P is the world relative price of clothing, or the terms of trade (evidently, there is only one world price).
Then at that new P, the foreign country does not produce clothing anymore. Why?

Because of the competitive conditions:

Pc (international) < $w^*.a^*(lc)$.

So the foreign country will specialize only in food.

It is important to be able to see that movement along a Ricardian production possibility frontier.

The home country does not produce food anymore but clothing.

So with trade we have,

$a(lc).w = Pc$ at home, while abroad: $a^*(lf).w^* = Pf$

Here, of course, Pc and Pf are the international prices.

And w/w^* = FACTORAL TERMS OF TRADE = $[Pc.(1/a(lc))]/[Pf.(1/a^*(lf))]$

Now, remember, if Pc/Pf increased (in other words, if there was an increase in the terms of trade), the home country gained (foreign country lost) in the exchange model.

It is still the case here.

Now let's go back to the case in which people express a relative high demand for clothing:

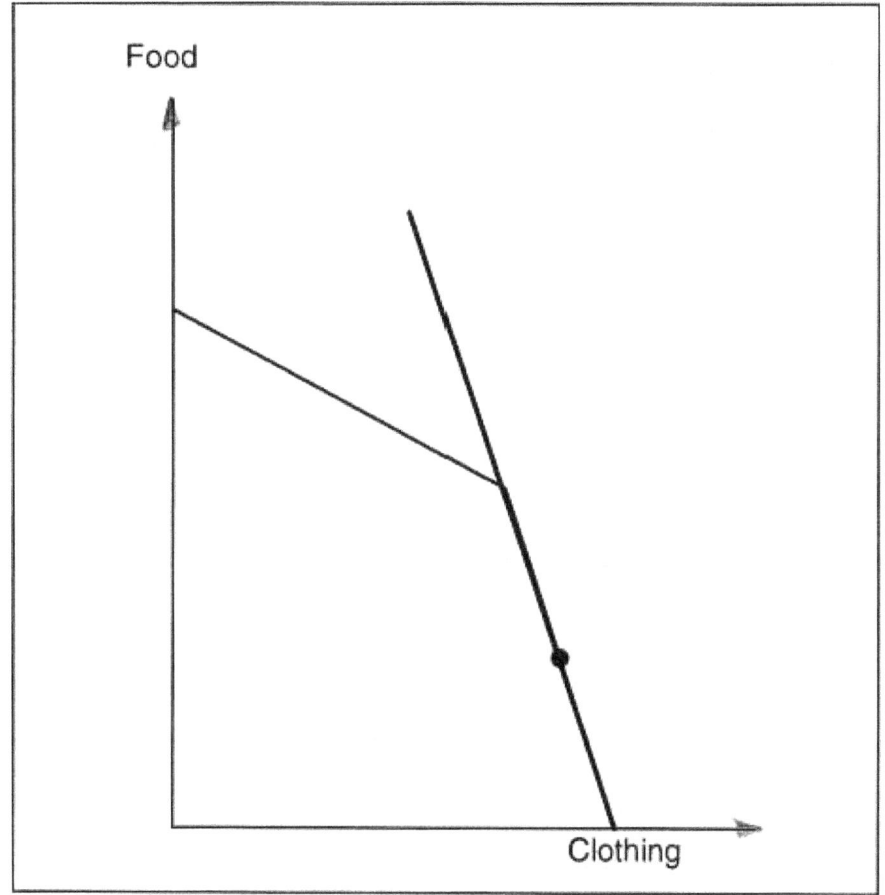

Then, in that special case, a(lc).w = Pc = a*(lc).w*

or, in other words, [1/a(lc)]/[1/a*(lc)] = w/w*

So in that case, w/w* depends only on the relative productivity of labor for that commodity.

Similarly, if the demand for food is very high ... we have that:

  w/w* = [1/a(lf)]/[1/a*(lf)]

Let's take an example:

a(lf) = 15 and a(lc) = 30   (at home)

a*(lf) = 5 and a*(lc) = 15   (abroad)

Here it is clear that the foreign country has an absolute advantage in both clothing and food, but it does not have a relative advantage in clothing. Because while its productivity is higher than the home country for food and for clothing, we still have:

a(lc)/a(lf) = 2 and a*(lc)/a*(lf) = 3.

Suppose also that the demand for clothing is relatively high, so that even the foreign country will produce some clothing -> what will the w/w* be?

Graphically this can be represented with the world transformation schedule:

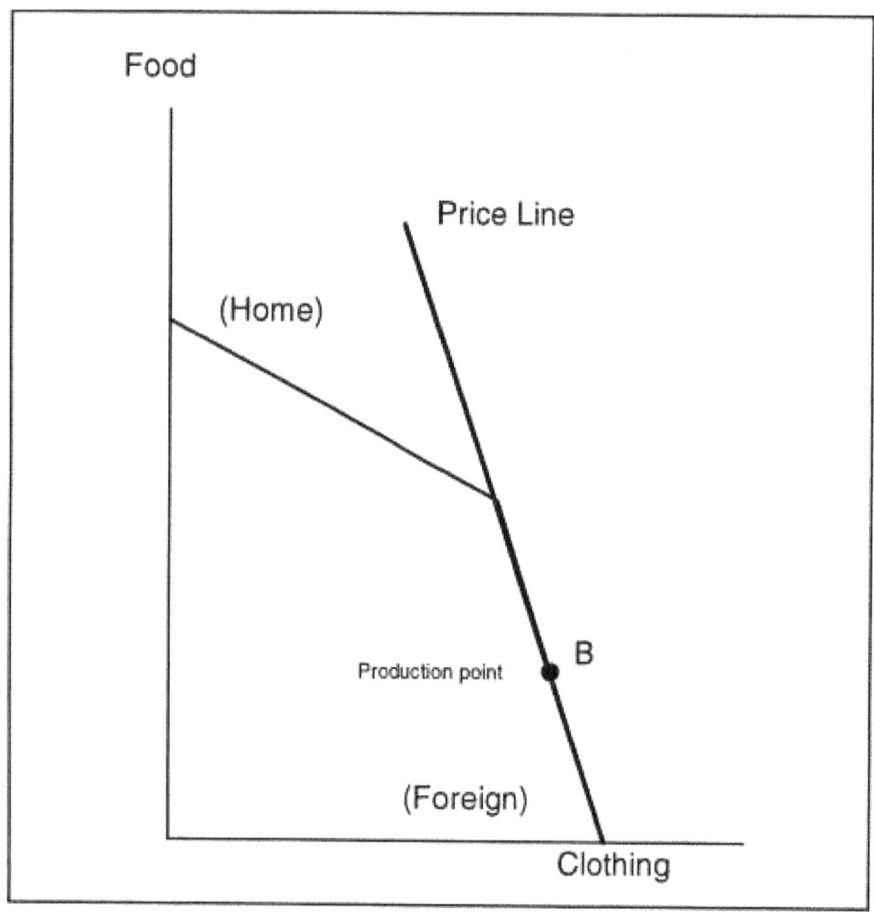

On that world production possibility schedule, we know that at B, the home AND the foreign countries are producing clothing. And we also know that there is only one world relative price (indicated by the slope of the price line):

Pc = a(lc).w = a*(lc).w*

Or, we can say that w/w* = productivity of the home country divided by the one of the foreign country.

With the number given, w/w* = (1/30)/(1/15) = 1/2. So note that when the two countries are producing the same good, the country with an absolute advantage in that good will have a higher salary ... even if this country does not have a relative advantage in that good!

So, to repeat, <u>when</u> a commodity is so in demand that it is produced by both countries, the factoral terms of trade w/w* is given by the ratio of labour productivities.

<u>In the other cases,</u> the factoral terms of trade is a function of productivity and prices.

Also if a country has an absolute advantage in both goods, it will still gain by importing the good for which it does not have a <u>comparative advantage.</u>

<u>Shocks and Income distribution:</u>

One of the characteristics of the Ricardian model is that it has a simple production structure. This can be represented --as you remember-- by a very simple production possibility frontier. This is why, it is sometimes used to study cases: ex. new technology and its impact.

In short, if there is a technological shock, could the country, that becomes more efficient, actually lose?

The answer is perhaps!

We know for sure that the world as a whole will win...

However, the distribution of this gain is NOT OBVIOUS.

To see that, let's make our usual assumptions:

 free trade world
 competition is at work
 2-country world

Here 5 commodities are produced.

Suppose home country produces commodities 1, 2 & 3 and foreign country produces commodities 4 & 5.

So that:

$a(l1)/a^*(l1) < a(l2)/a^*(l2) < a(l3)/a^*(l3) < a(l4)/a^*(l4) < a(l5)/a^*(l5)$.

So, the home country has a comparative advantage in goods 1, 2 and 3 over goods 4 and 5.

Through competition mechanisms, we know that in free trade, we will have:

$$\begin{cases} a(l1).w = P1 \\ a(l2).w = P2 \\ a(l3).w = P3 \\ a^*(l4).w^* = P4 \\ a^*(l5).w^* = P5 \end{cases}$$

Now suppose a technological breakthrough: for instance a(l1) goes down, so the number of hours of labour needed to produce one unit of good 1 decreases.

Because cornpetition is at work, P1 will go down:

$$P1 = a(l1).w$$

and for simplicity, suppose P2, P3 stay the same.

What is happening to the prices abroad?

. 3 cases are possible:

1st case: P4 and P5 stay unchanged:

If both countries produce commodity 3, ...

$$w.a(l3) = P3 = w^*.a^*(l3)$$

This means that cost structures of both countries are interlocked. And that result will allow us to show that P4 and P5 might stay the same (because in our assumption P2 and P3 stay unchanged.)

To see that mechanism, note:

$$P2 = a(l2).w$$
$$P3 = a(l3).w = a^*(l3).w^*$$

This means that w* stays unchanged, and by extension P4 and P5 stay unchanged:

$$P4 = a^*(l4).w^*$$
$$P5 = a^*(l5).w^*$$

So both countries benefit from the technology improvement (in proportion to their consumption) (because wage rates are not changed).

2nd case:

Foreign prices rise (and thus will foreign wage). Why: as P1 goes down, people consume more good 1. But as P1 decreases, there is also an income effect. Now if good 1 and good 4 & 5 are complementary, the demand for these 2 goods goes up, and prices of good 4 & 5 might rise by so much that the country can actually lose (cf. immiserizing growth).

3rd case: P4, P5 go down:

Why is it also possible?

If good 1 and good 4 & 5 are very good substitute...

$a^*(l4).w^* = P4$ and $a^*(l5).w^* = P5$

So if P4 or P5 goes down, w^* will follow.

In conclusion, the final impact of technological progress is quite difficult to assess, despite the fact we are using one the simplest model on earth...

The non traded goods:

Before: conventional wisdom was that goods were traded, while services were not.

But now: We talk a lot about trade in services: - banking and financial services, insurance, tourism, marketing ... It is one of the hottest topics in trade negotiations today. In short, industrial world wants to have free trade in services, but third world is not too keen about it: role of comparative advantages!

However, it is still relevant to make a distinction between traded and non-traded commodities. So to be very general, see a good or a service that is non-traded as if its transportation cost was infinite.

In the Ricardian model, it is VERY simple: we know the no-profit condition and we can't escape it!

$$Pn = a(ln).w$$

and as with any technological coefficient, $a(ln)$ is given

so w will be the key: But w is given by $a(l_1).w = P_1$

If P_1 is known from the international market, we do know w, as a result of that -because we know $a(l_n)$- we can find P_n.

So if we separate commodities in traded and non-traded, we can allocate L (Total available supply of labor):

$L = a(l_t).X_t + a(l_n).X_n$

On the next graph, we represent the choice facing an economy between tradable and non tradable goods.

We will see, in the second part of this course, that its is very worthwhile to study that aspect of an economy.

$P.X_T$ = value (on the world market - world price) of the production of tradable goods in **S**.

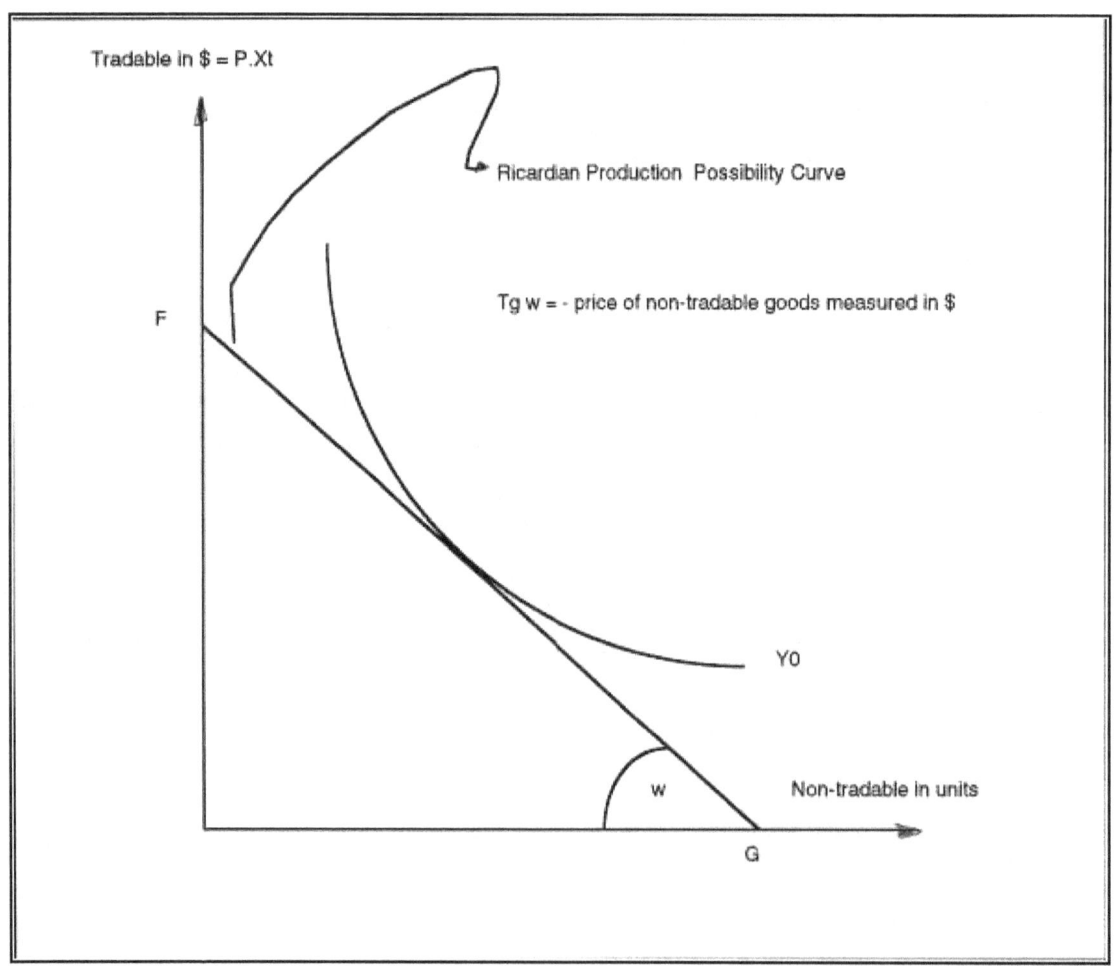

At F, all the labour is used to produce tradable goods. We are at a balanced trade point! Why? Because we are on the PPF. In a similar way, at G, we are in a situation where all the labor is used to produce non-tradables. However, on this graph, the observed optimum is at A.

Now:

if $a(l_i)$ goes down, so that $P_i/a(l_i) > P_j/a(l_j)$
then we don't produce good j anymore. But we still produce N the non traded good.

In short: before: we produced and traded good J -
produced good N -

Now, because $P_i/a(l_i) > P_j/a(l_j)$, we give up entirely the production of good j, we start the production of good i (that we can trade) and we KEEP the production of good N.

Another point worth noting, is what happens when the demand for our product, at the international level, increases:

this is reflected in a change in the slope of the (value)PPF:

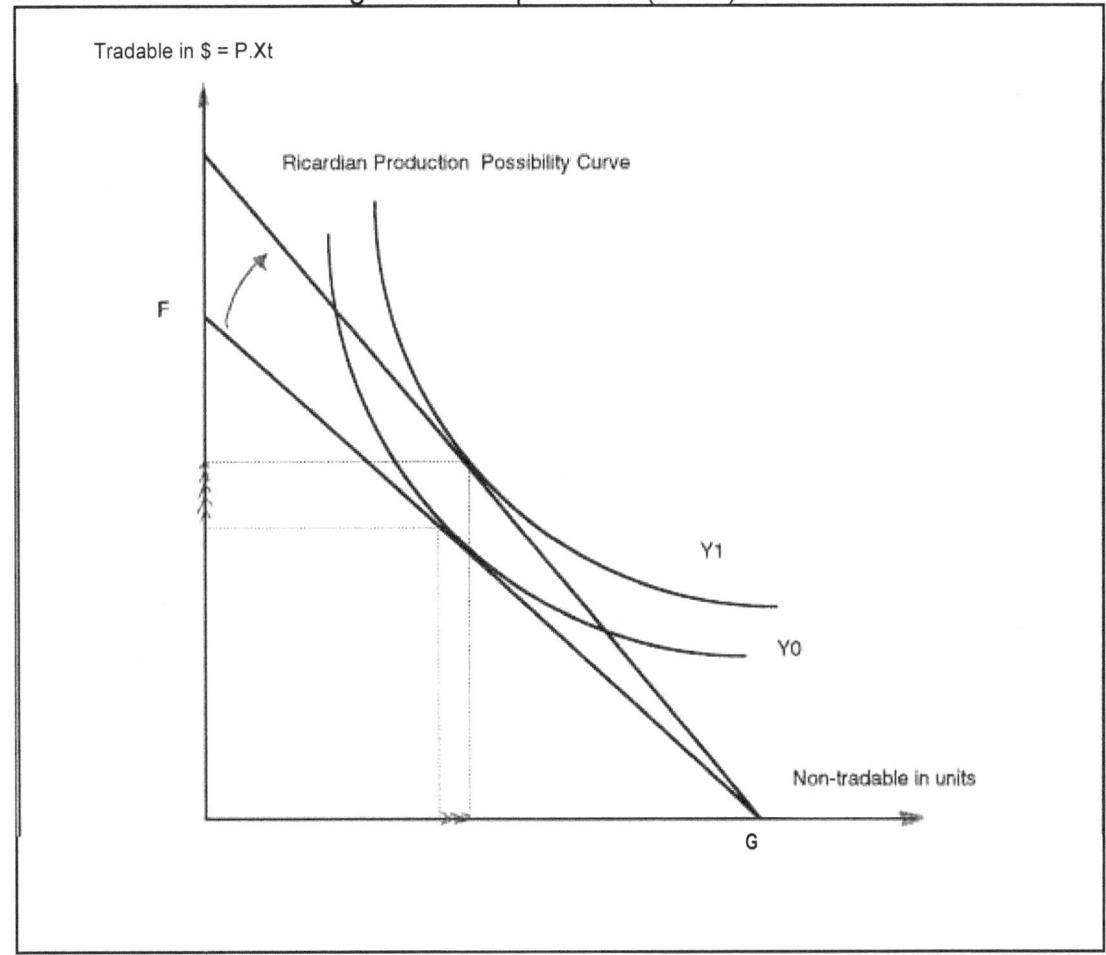

E: THE SPECIFIC FACTOR MODEL AND INCOME DISTRIBUTION:

Basic idea:

If production technology is too rigid, we cannot explain how certain factor of production will lose or gain from policies enacted by GVT. With a specific factor, which is a more powerful model, it is possible ... Some economists and political scientists use that kind of models to do just that and present a public choice view of trade.

Before starting this chapter, let's differentiate between **technology** and **technique:**

> A **technology** represents the state of knowledge for efficient combinations of K and L (at every level of w and r).
> A **technique** represents one efficient way of combining K an L (i.e.: for a given w/r).
> The analogy to remember is: **technology is like a menu** at a restaurant, and **technique is one item on that menu.** If you hear that two countries share the same technology, they might have different techniques.

First, the competitive firm:

Remember that, in General Equilibrium, competitive means, among other things, Profit = Total Revenue - Total Cost = P.Q - w.L -r.K =0
For if this was not the case, if profit was greater than 0 , we would have to explain why...

Let's assume CRTS. What is the precise definition of Constant return to scale? Remember that CRTS is compatible with diminishing returns.

Isoquant and Isocost lines.

We saw, in our second lecture, that with a CRTS, the PPf was concave to the origin because it was more efficient to produce a mix of F, C with only one technique.

Now, we can explain why: the reason is diminishing marginal rate of substitution between inputs.

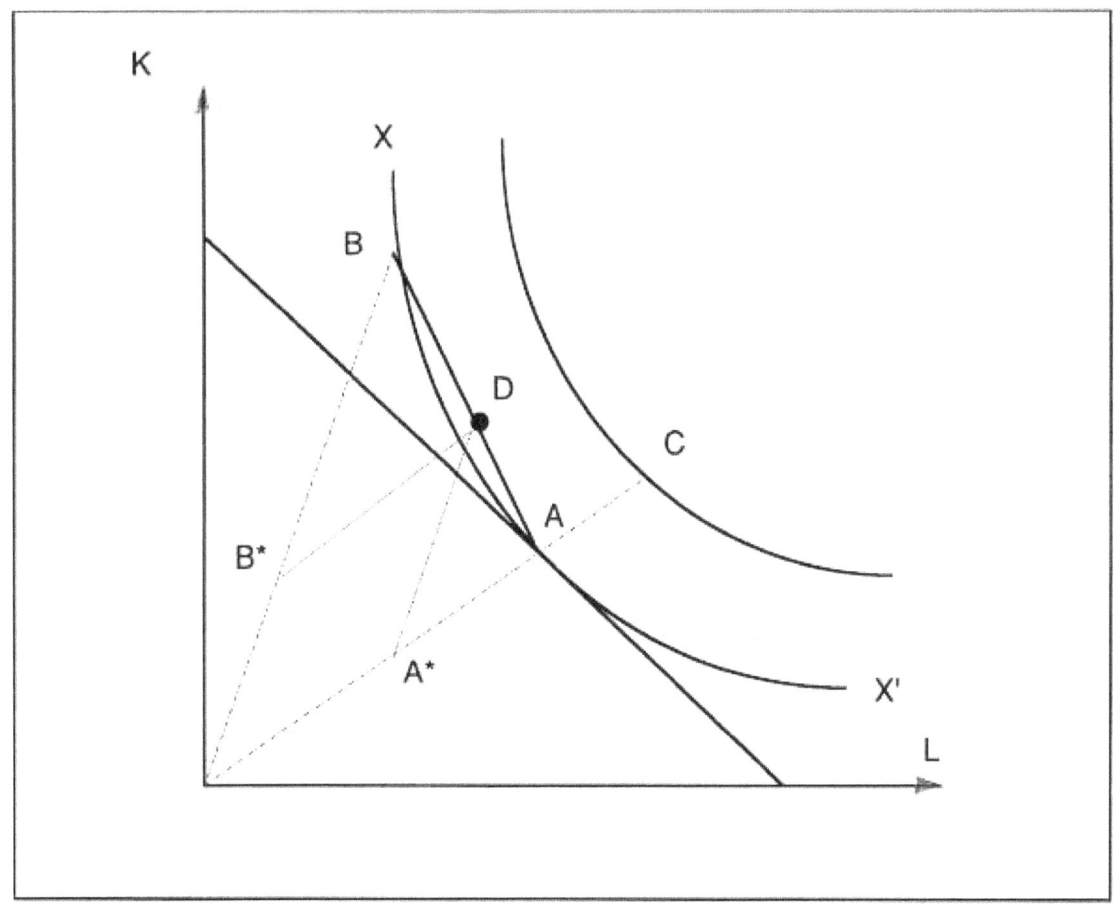

With that isoquant XX', we can see that it is possible to produce one unit of good at A or B.

Because of CRTS, we know that if we use half of the input of (K,L) that we are using at A, we would produce half of a unit of output: at A: (KA,LA) gives one unit, and at A* (KA/2,LA/2) gives 1/2 unit. Similarly, when we are at B*, we use half of the capital and half of the labor used at B, we produce half of a unit of output. In order to produce one unit of output we could combine two techniques (i.e. two K/L ratios) and do a vectorial summation of B* and A*. This would lead us to point D.

So when we <u>add</u> the inputs from B* and A* we reach D, which is equal to B,A in terms of production (one unit), but is inefficient in terms of use of capital and labor.

This is why it never pays to use 2 techniques in a production function characterized by decreasing MRTS...

Let us introduce pure competition and the specific factor.

L = labor supply = Lc + Lf = Labor demand.

Fixed supply and no unemployment. Why?

W adjusts in such a way that there is a full employment of factors of production. So, in these kind of models, if you see unemployment, then you have to explain why markets do not clear.

(In this course, we will assume that there are no factors preventing markets to clear). Kind of Walrasian equilibrium.

K = capital = Kc [our specific factor for clothing.]

T = land = Tf [our specific factor for food]

Again what we have here is full employment of the specific factors: supply = demand.

There are two ways to introduce a specific facto in a model,

a- It is equivalent to imagine that the cost of moving K from one sector to another is <u>infinite</u> (also for T).

b- Alternatively, one can view the specific factor model as a short term version of a more general version of the production (the famous "two by two by two". (cf. Chapter F)).

Whatever the justification chosen, we can now introduce the competitive profit conditions:

Denote: w as the wage rate (which is the return on the common factor), rk as the rental on capital (= return on K) and rt as the rental on land (= return on land)

Again we have our usual 2 goods, Food and Clothing.

Food requires land and labour.
Clothing requires capital and labour.

Note that WF = WC, this means that labour shifts effortlessly from the food sector to the clothing sector so as to equate the wage in both sectors.

So the core of the specific factor model is that these 2 economic sectors will compete for the common factor: labour. And of course, their ability to compete for this factor will depend on PC/PF so ultimately it will depend on <u>taste.</u>

The competitive profit conditions are:

$$a(lc).w + a(kc).rk = Pc$$
$$a(lf).w + a(tf).rt = Pf$$

[where a(lc) = number of units of labour needed in the production of 1 unit of clothing].

Similarly, a(ij) is the number of units of i to produce one unit of j.

Given the shape of the production, the w/rt and the w/rk, the technique is chosen so as to minimize cost:

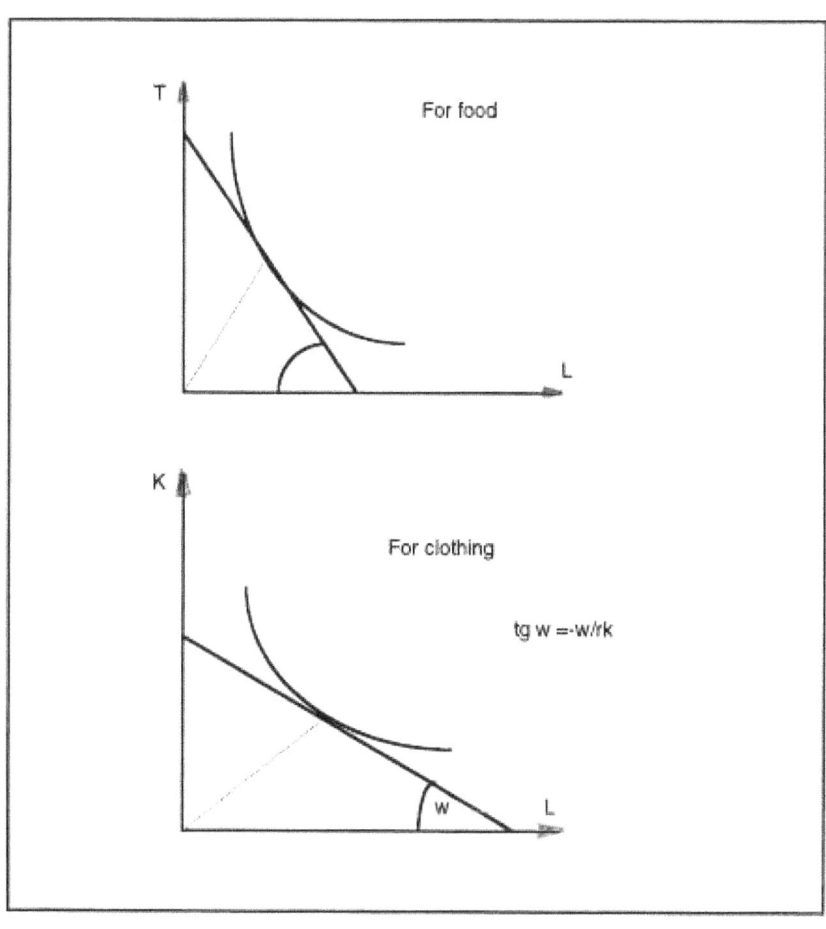

So at the point of cost minimization slope of the isocost = slope of isoquant: -w/rk = da(kc)/da(lc) = a negative number =tg w.

Note that a(lc) = L/Xc and a(kc) = K/Xc

So K/L = a(kc)/a(lc), which is NOT a constant so dK/dL = K/L.
But dK/dL = da(kc)/da(lc)

So at the optimum we have:

w.da(lc) + rk.da(kc) = O.   [I]

What does it mean? At the optimum, we can't reduce cost and at the same time produce the same amount as before.

Defining,

$$\begin{cases} \theta_{LC} = w \cdot a(lc)/Pc & \text{[the labor cost share of clothing, } < 1 \text{]} \\ \theta_{KC} = rk \cdot a(kc)/Pc & \text{[the capital cost share of clothing, } < 1 \text{]} \end{cases}$$

Similarly, for food we have, θ_{LF} and θ_{TF}

And $\theta_{LC} + \theta_{KC} = 1 = \theta_{LF} + \theta_{TF}$.

Remember that $\hat{a}_{LC} = da(lc)/a(lc)$

So equation [I] becomes after some substitutions,

$$\begin{cases} \theta_{LC} \cdot \hat{a}_{LC} + \theta_{KC} \cdot \hat{a}_{KC} = 0 \\ \theta_{LF} \cdot \hat{a}_{LF} + \theta_{TF} \cdot \hat{a}_{TF} = 0 \end{cases}$$

These equations tell you that --at the optimum-- the relative change in cost from substituting one technique for another (changing input) is = 0.

Let us differentiate the 2 following equations:

$$\begin{cases} a(lc) \cdot w + a(kc) \cdot rk = Pc \\ a(lf) \cdot w + a(tf) \cdot rt = Pf \end{cases}$$

We have:

$$\begin{cases} da(lc) \cdot w + a(lc) \cdot \mathbf{dw} + da(kc) \cdot rk + a(kc) \cdot \mathbf{drk} = \mathbf{dPc} \\ da(lf) \cdot w + a(lf) \cdot \mathbf{dw} + da(tf) \cdot rt + a(tf) \cdot \mathbf{drt} = \mathbf{dPf} \end{cases}$$

But, because we are at the optimum, we have the following relationships:

$$\begin{cases} w \cdot da(lc) + rk \cdot da(kc) = 0 \\ w \cdot da(lf) + rt \cdot da(tf) = 0 \end{cases}$$

So the differentiation becomes:

$$\begin{cases} a(lc) \cdot \mathbf{dw} + a(kc) \cdot \mathbf{drk} = \mathbf{dPc} \\ a(lf) \cdot \mathbf{dw} + a(tf) \cdot \mathbf{drt} = \mathbf{dPf} \end{cases}$$

Dividing both sides of each equation by P's:

$$\begin{cases} a(lc).dw/Pc + a(kc).drk/Pc = dPc/Pc = \hat{P}_C \\ a(lf).dw/Pf + a(tf).dtf/Pf = dPf/Pf = \hat{P}_F \end{cases}$$

Multiply and divide by w and r (rk or rt):

$$\begin{cases} [a(lc).w/Pc].[dw/w] + [a(kc).rk/Pc].[drk/rk] = \hat{P}_C \\ [a(lf).w/Pf].[dw/w] + [a(tf).rt/Pf].[drt/rt] = \hat{P}_F \end{cases}$$

$$\begin{cases} \theta_{LC}.\hat{w} + \theta_{KC}.\hat{r}_K = \hat{P}_C \\ \theta_{LF}.\hat{w} + \theta_{TF}.\hat{r}_T = \hat{P}_F \end{cases} \qquad [\text{II}]$$

This system of equations [II] is crucial to understand general equilibrium:

First application: Suppose Pc increases but Pf stay the same.

Also, suppose that θ_{LC}, θ_{KC}, θ_{LF} and θ_{TF}, the distributive shares remain the same.

$$\begin{cases} \theta_{LC}.\hat{w} + \theta_{KC}.\hat{r}_K = \hat{P}_C = 10\% \text{ (for instance)} \\ \theta_{LF}.\hat{w} + \theta_{TF}.\hat{r}_T = \hat{P}_F = 0 \end{cases}$$

As a result [proof below], we will have --given that $\hat{L}$ is equal to 0:

$$\hat{r}_K > \hat{P}_C > \hat{w} > \hat{P}_F(=0) > \hat{r}_T$$

It is clear, because $\hat{P}_F = 0$, that landlords are losing.

Second application of the system of equations [II]:

If, as a result of immigration, w decreases, and $\hat{P}_C = \hat{P}_F = 0$,

we will have $\hat{r}_T$ and $\hat{r}_K > 0$. In other words, landlords and capitalists are gaining.

We assume full <u>employment of factors of production</u>:

so it means that a(kc).Xc = K and a(tf).Xf = T
(demand for capital equals supply of capital, demand for land equals supply of land).

L? Slightly more complicated because it is used by food and clothing.

a(lc).Xc + a(lf).Xf = L
[demand for labor = supply of labor]

But we know that Xc = K/a(kc) and Xf = T/a(tf), so we replace:

a(lc).[K/a(kc)] + a(lf).[T/a(tf)] = L   [III]

The equation [III] must be met to ensure full employment of all three factors of production at the same time.

To see how --by what mechanism-- this is possible, suppose we are at full employment, and K, T stay the same but there is an increase in L (cf. immigration):

K.d[a(lc)/a(kc)] + T.d[a(lf)/a(tf)] = dL

Divide by L on both sides and multiply and divide on the LHS by [a(lc)/a(kc)] and [a(lf)/a(tf)]:

$$\frac{K.[a_{LC}/a_{KC}].d[a_{LC}/a_{KC}]}{[a_{LC}/a_{KC}].L} + \frac{T.[a_{LF}/a_{TF}].d[a_{LF}/a_{TF}]}{[a_{LF}/a_{TF}].L} = dL/L = \hat{L}$$

Using the "^" notation,

$(K/L).[a_{LC}/a_{KC}].[\hat{a}_{LC} - \hat{a}_{KC}] + (T/L).[a_{LF}/a_{TF}].[\hat{a}_{LF} - \hat{a}_{TF}] = \hat{L}$

But $K/a_{KC} = X_C$ and $T/a_{TF} = X_F$.

Thus, we have:

$X_C.(a_{LC}/L).[\hat{a}_{LC} - \hat{a}_{KC}] + X_F.(a_{LF}/L).[\hat{a}_{LF} - \hat{a}_{TF}] = \hat{L}$

But, $X_C.a_{LC} = L_C$ and $X_F.a_{LF} = L_F$.

Defining $\lambda_{LC} = \dfrac{L_C}{L}$ and $\lambda_{LF} = \dfrac{L_F}{L}$, we finally have:

$\lambda_{LC}.[\hat{a}_{LC} - \hat{a}_{KC}] + \lambda_{LF}.[\hat{a}_{LF} - \hat{a}_{TF}] = \hat{L}$ (IV)

So this means that as L goes up, a(lc) and a(lf) rise --while a(kc) and a(kf) decrease-- and this is weighted by the relative share in industries. (remember: $\lambda_{LC} + \lambda_{LF} = 1$)

How is wage determined? Key concept: diminishing returns. Remember, the concept of diminishing return is very different from the concept of diminishing return to scale.

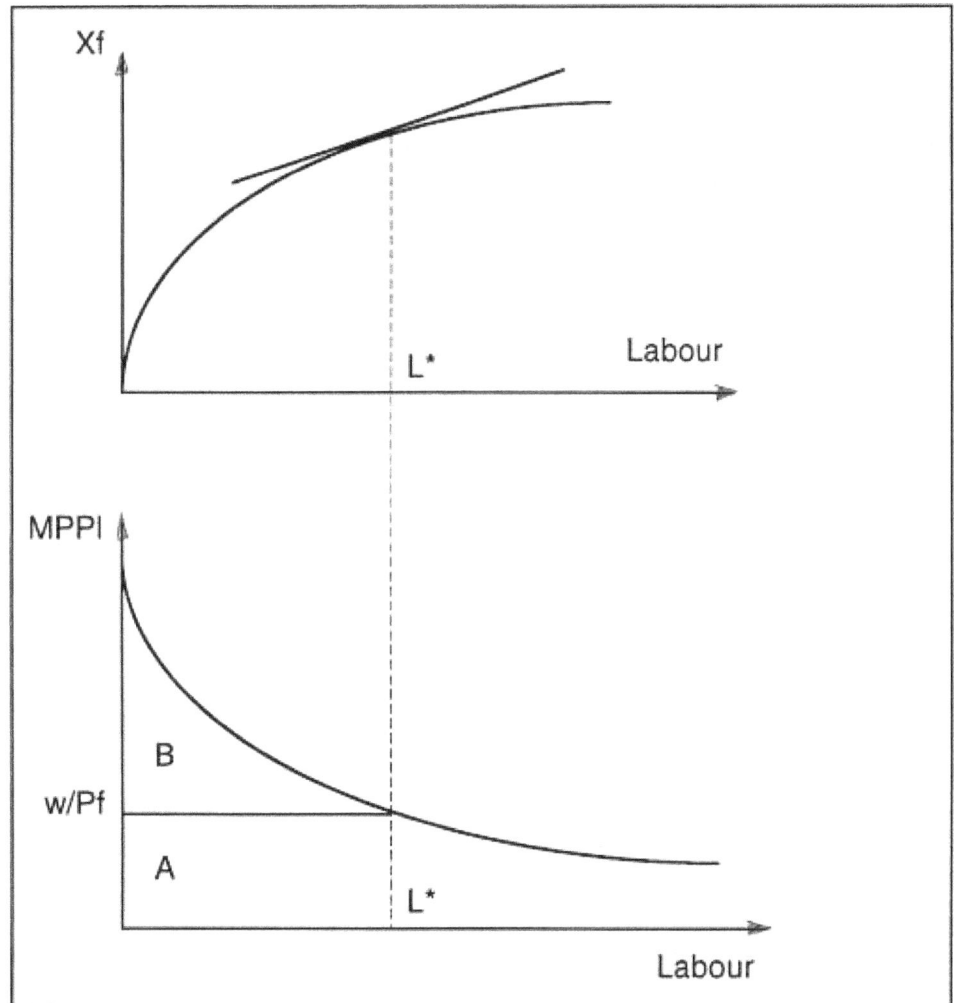

Comment: B = return on land and A = return on labour.

Deriving the PPF with the assumptions of diminishing returns, constant return to scale, 1 common factor (L) and two specific factors (T and K):

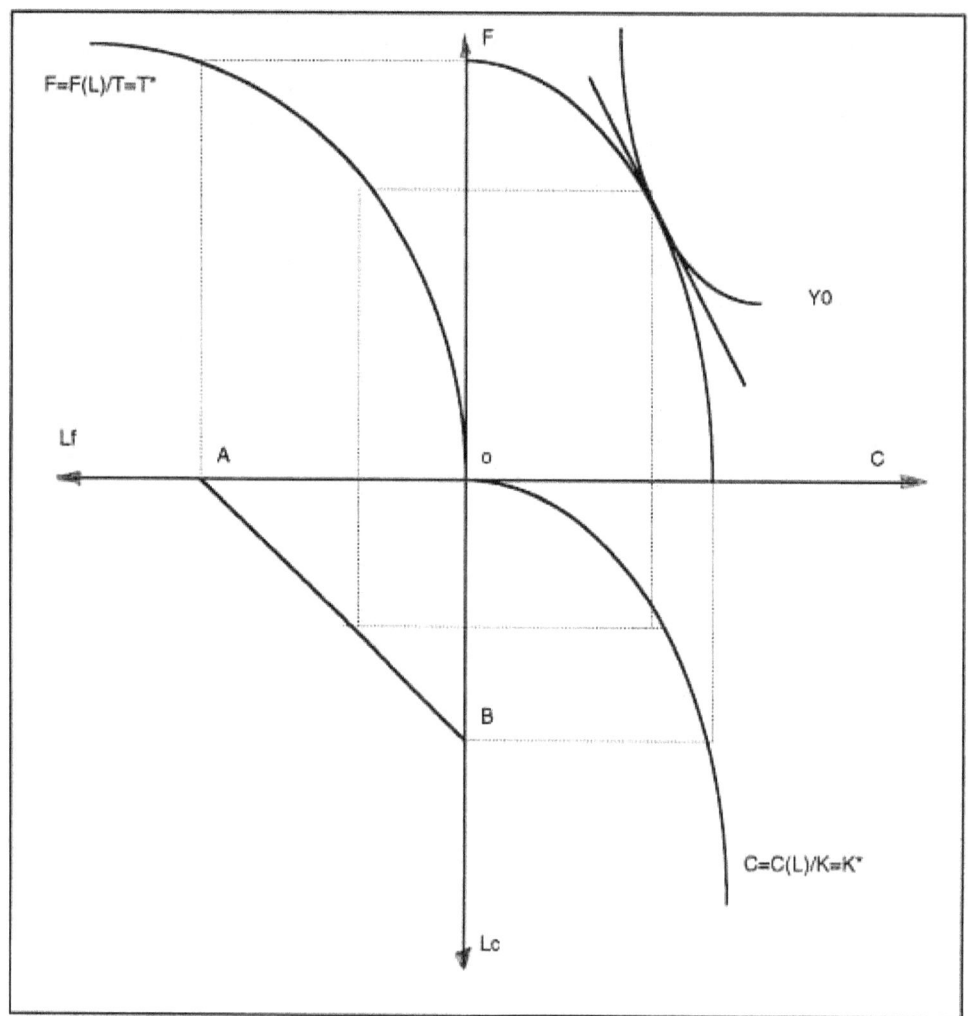

Comments: OA = 1OB != L = Total Labour. This graph tells us that taste and technology and endowment simultaneously determine: w, rk, rt, Lc, Lf, Pc/Pf, Xf and Xc (and YO).

Another to study the situation is to look at the competition for the mobile factor:

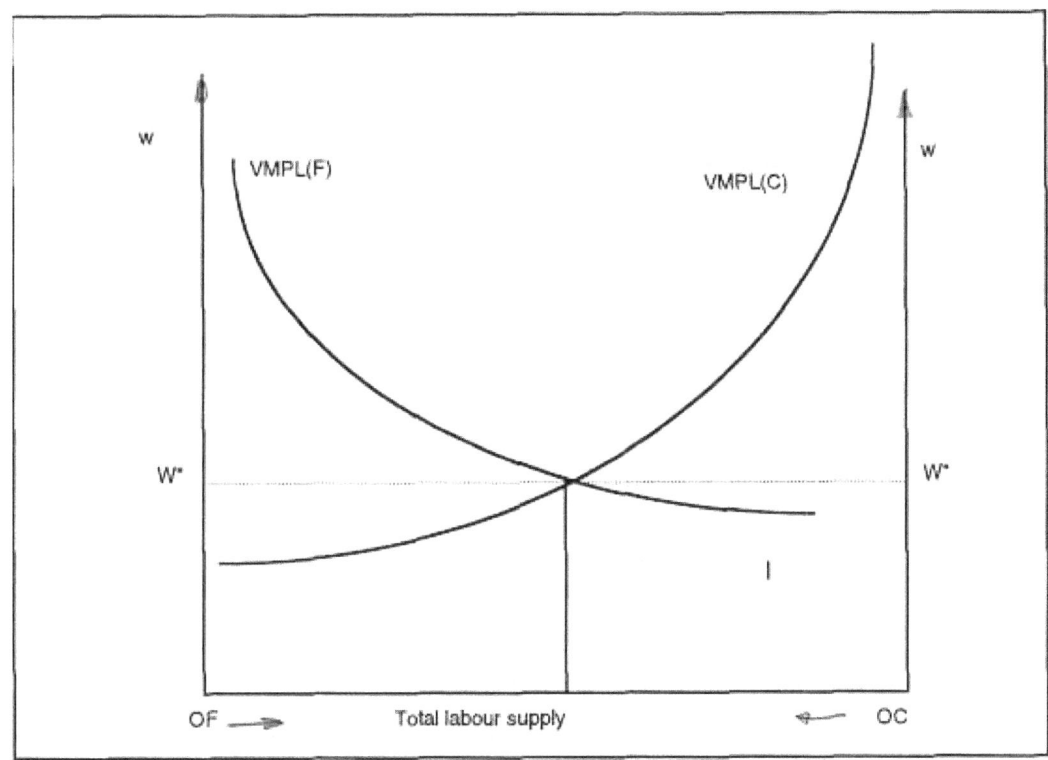

We can now continue our demonstration:

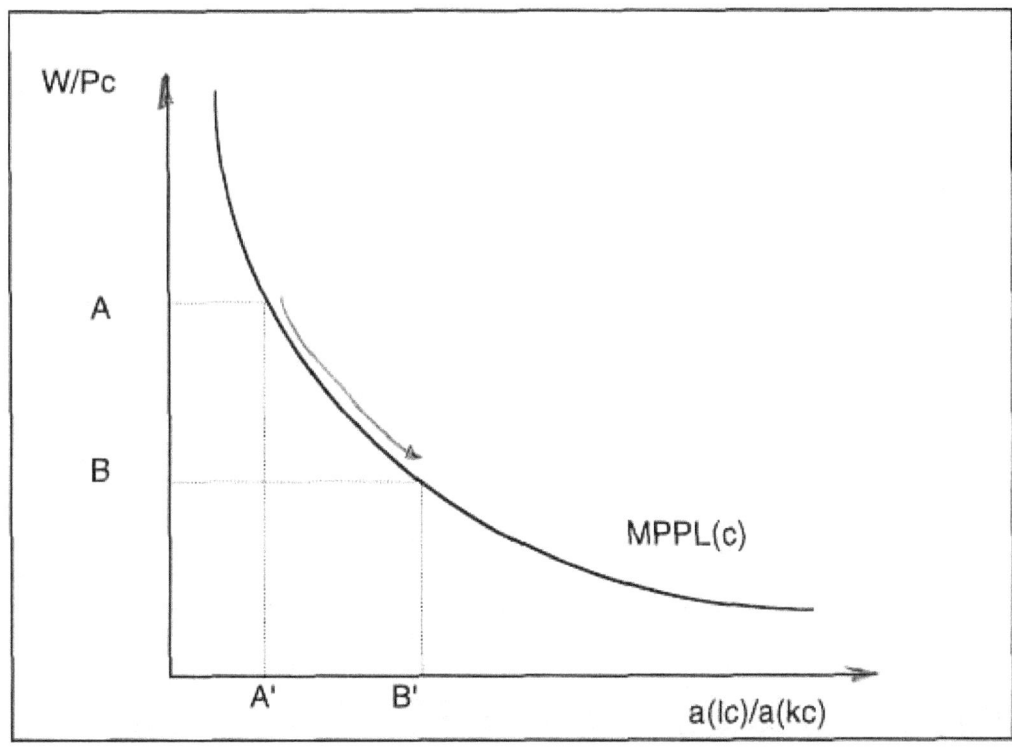

Now defining elasticity of labour marginal product:

$$\begin{cases} \gamma_{LC} = -[\hat{a}_{LC} - \hat{a}_{KC}]/(\hat{w} - \hat{p}_C) \\ \gamma_{LF} = -[\hat{a}_{LF} - \hat{a}_{TF}]/(\hat{w} - \hat{p}_F) \end{cases}$$

These two elasticities tell us how techniques change as real wage increases. Replacing in equation (IV) (in these notes: p.55) gives us:

$$\lambda_{LC} \cdot \gamma_{LC} \cdot (\hat{w} - \hat{p}_C) + \lambda_{LF} \cdot \gamma_{LF} \cdot (\hat{w} - \hat{p}_F) = -\hat{L}$$

$$\hat{w} = \beta_C \cdot \hat{P}_C + \beta_F \cdot \hat{P}_F - 1/\gamma \cdot \hat{L} \qquad (V)$$

where $\beta_C = \lambda_{LC} \cdot \gamma_{LC}/\gamma$ and $\beta_F = \lambda_{LF} \cdot \gamma_{LF}/\gamma$ ($\beta_C + \beta_F = 1$)
and $\gamma = \lambda_{LC} \cdot \gamma_{LC} + \lambda_{LF} \cdot \gamma_{LF}$ (this is the weighted average of the MPLelasticities)

The equation (V) deserves some comments.

If γ is large, then for a certain $\hat{w}$, we will have a large percentage decrease in L. (given $\hat{P}_C = \hat{P}_F = 0$).
Also, if γ is large, a certain % increase in L will not lead to a large % decrease in w.

Now, if L is fixed, this means that $\hat{w}$ will be trapped between $\hat{P}_C$ and $\hat{P}_F$.

Now remember the 2 equations:

$$\begin{cases} \theta_{LC} \cdot \hat{w} + \theta_{KC} \cdot \hat{r}_K = \hat{P}_C = 10\% \text{ (for instance)} \\ \theta_{LF} \cdot \hat{w} + \theta_{TF} \cdot \hat{r}_T = \hat{P}_F = 0 \end{cases}$$

As a result, given that $\hat{L}$ is equal to 0,:

$$\hat{r}_K > \hat{P}_C > \hat{w} > \hat{P}_F (=0) > \hat{r}_T$$

Suppose k=10% and P_F = 0%,

we know that w will be between 0 and 10%.

So the return on the factor specifically used will go up by a magnified amount...

But the return on the factor for which P decreases, will go down by a magnified amount!

So now, we can use this model to make prediction about the likely effects of an opening to trade with rest of the world.

We know that trade will change relative prices:

Pf will go up or down, Pc will go down or up ...

So there will be an income redistribution.   What about w?

If Pf/Pc decreases, we know that landlords are losing big... But what about labour? The answer is "uncertain!" ... Why?

We know that Pf/Pc decreases, but real wage in terms of clothing will go down, while real wage in terms of food will go up! So if food is a large part of the budget, the real wage of the worker will go up (but if not, the real wage of the worker will go down).

This uncertainty concerning the fate of workers is called:
"...neoclassical ambiguity" (Journal of Economic Theory 1977).

Note that the opening to free trade has unambiguous effects on the returns of the specific factors.

Here it seems that a GVT could affect the standard of living of a certain pressure group (i.e. landlord or capitalist) with tariffs. But labour would not react too much because it would be divided ... (cf. M. OLSON: "The Logic of Collective Action").

This is a new branch of international trade theory: "endogenous trade theory". (cf. Public Choice).

Growth:

Suppose a small country, which can not influence the relative world prices. So we have What is happening if this country experiences growth?

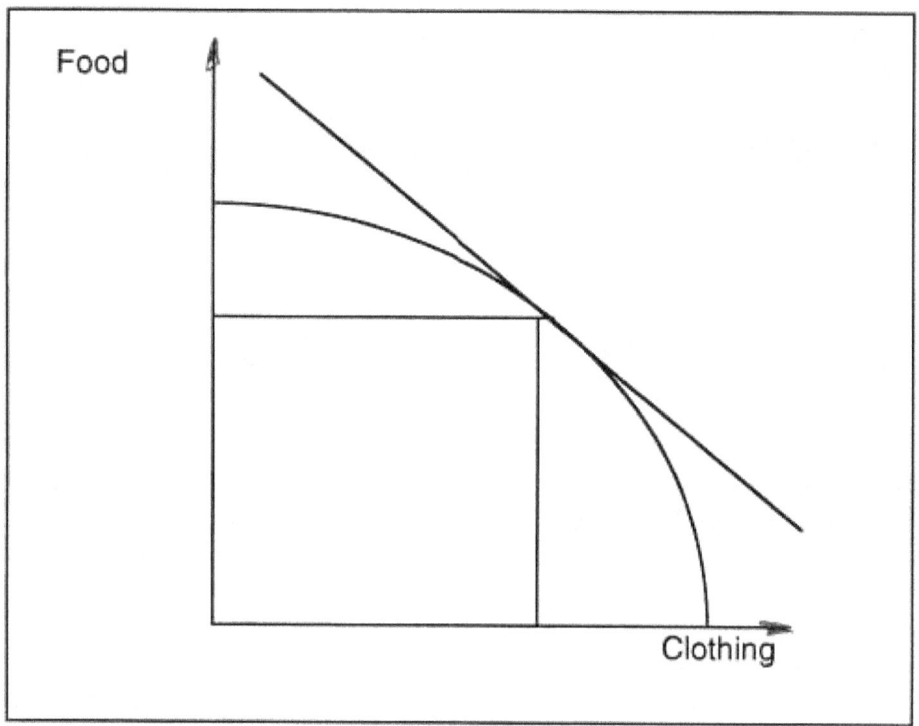

There are 3 possible cases:

1 - balanced growth
2 - growth in one of its specific factor (here, land)
3 - growth in the common factor (labour)

1. **if it is a balanced growth,** nothing special happens because the world price is fixed: it is just an outward shift of the PPF, and rt, rk and w stay constant:

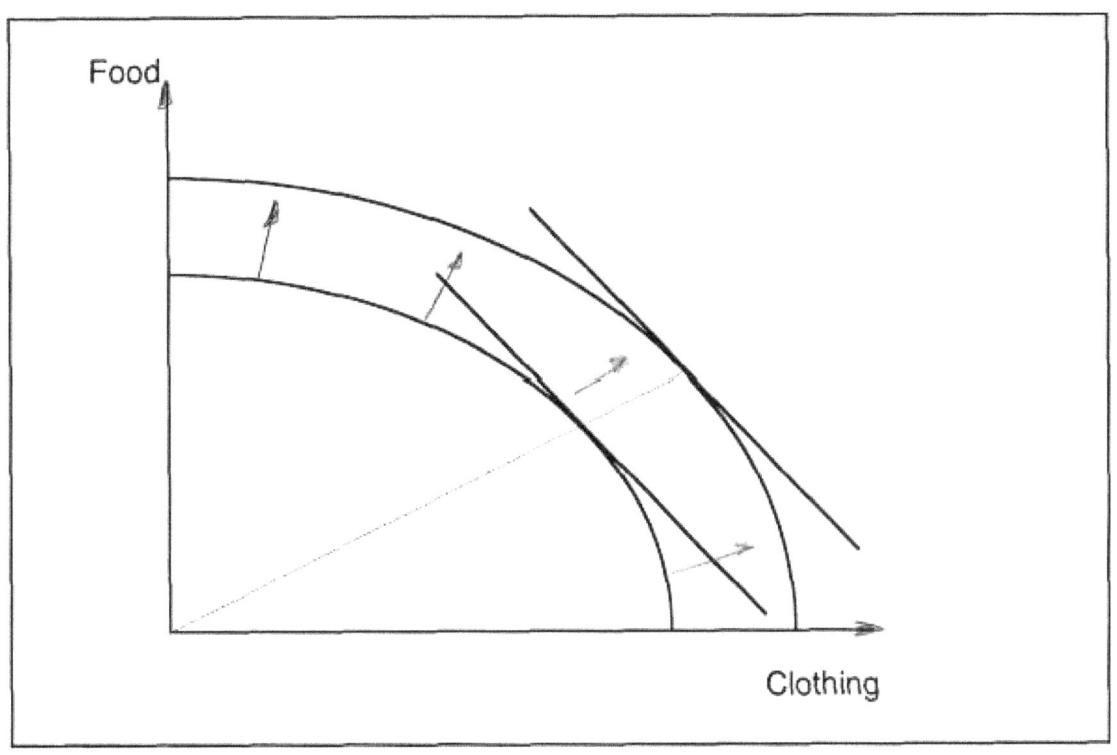

if it is in its specific factor, for instance land:

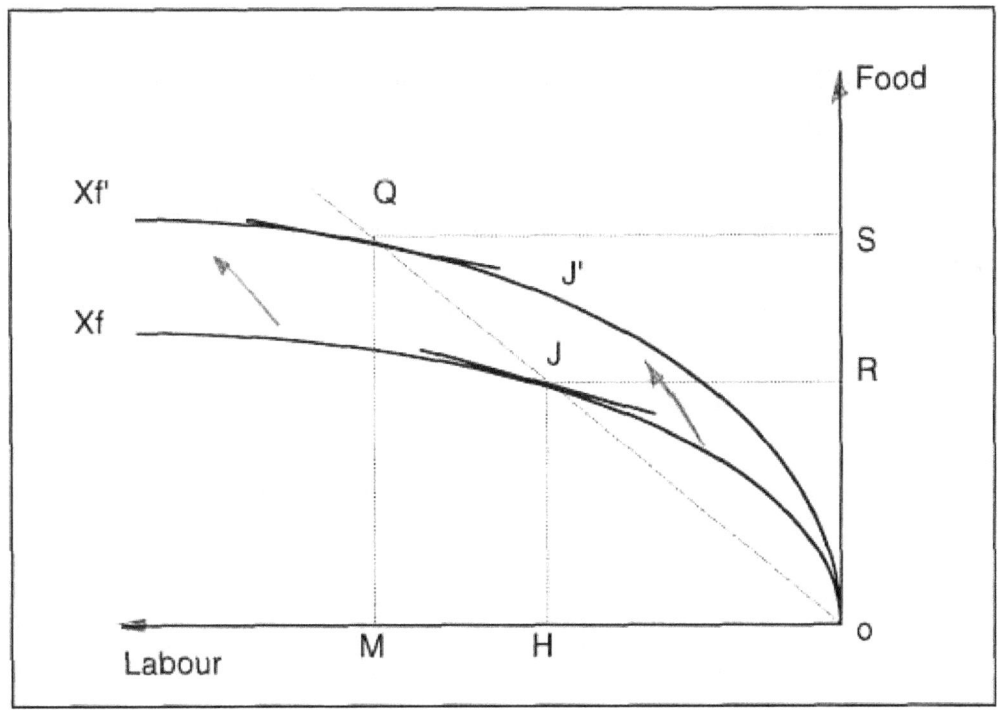

Suppose land has increased 50%, so at every value of labour, MPLabour is greater than before.

Now, what about output?

We mentioned CRTS. So if labour increases also by 50%, we will have a 50% increase in output: $\|OS\| = 1.5 \cdot \|OR\|$ when $\|OM\| = 1.5 \cdot \|OH\|$

Now slopes at Q and J are the same. So labour will be attracted in the food sector: from A to B:

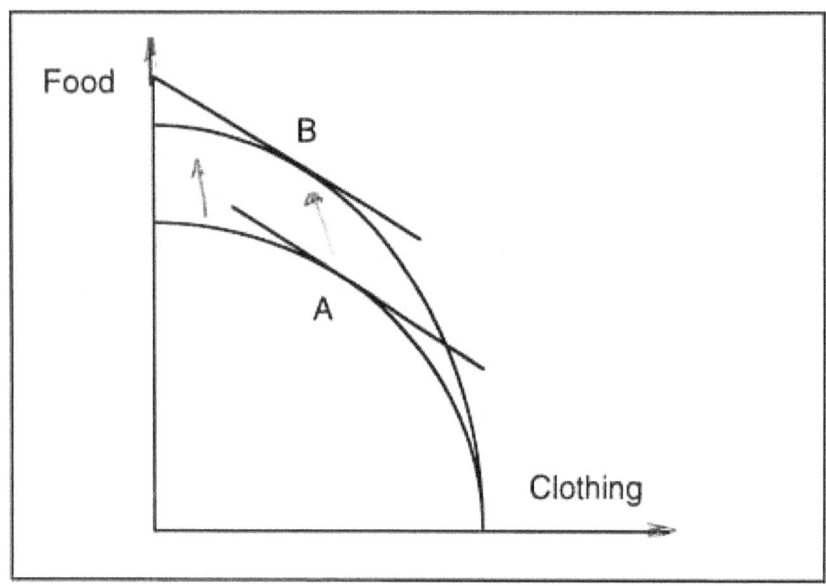

Note, BECAUSE THIS IS A SMALL COUNTRY, slopes at A and B are the same. Why? Same relative world prices as before. So as a result of growth in land, output of food goes up, while output of clothing decreases:

Lf goes up, Lc goes down, w goes up and rt goes down (because, at the new output the labour/Land ratio is lower)

What about rk?

It goes down - unambiguously! Why?

Because $a(lc).\hat{w} + a(kc).\hat{r}_K = \hat{P}_C = 0$

3. **growth in the common factor**:

Labour goes up. But $\hat{P}_C = \hat{P}_F = 0$

So w goes down, but rk and rt go up because MPK and MPT go up.

There will be expansion of BOTH output (probably not in the same proportions).

So the conclusions are:

A. if commodity prices stay the same, then if there is a rise in factors of production,
when w goes up, rk and rt go down
w goes down, rk and rt go up.

B. if endowments remain the same but Pc/Pf changes then

$r_K > P_C > W > P_F (=O) > r_T$

Trade and the specific factor model:

Remember we could have trade as long as relative foreign price in autarky is different from home price in autarky.

3 reasons are possible to justify this initial difference with this model:

- **different tastes**
- **different technologies**
- **different endoitements.**

Please note that concerning tastes, it is often assumed that they are different and that we should not quarrel about them, example "French people like wine but Canadian people like beer". Now, there is a famous article by G. Stigler and G. Becker, from the AER March 1977, (Vol. 67 nr 2, pp 76-90 -- highly recommended): "De Gustibus Non Est Disputandum", that proposes to reverse that basic idea, and that in fact tastes are the same ... but relative costs are different.

This can be illustrated with the following example: we observe that there are more swimming pools in California than in Alaska; does that mean that people from Alaska do not like swimming as much as the Californians?

The Dutch disease:

In the Netherlands, export sector is big (natural gas and "other exports").

As the price of natural gas went up, the quantity exported of gas went up, pushing the wage up. By doing so, it raised the labor cost of the "other exports" (whose prices were constant (S - S1), p = p*).

So the return on the specific factor in the "other exports" went down. This is called the Dutch Disease, a "crowding out effect" of some sort.

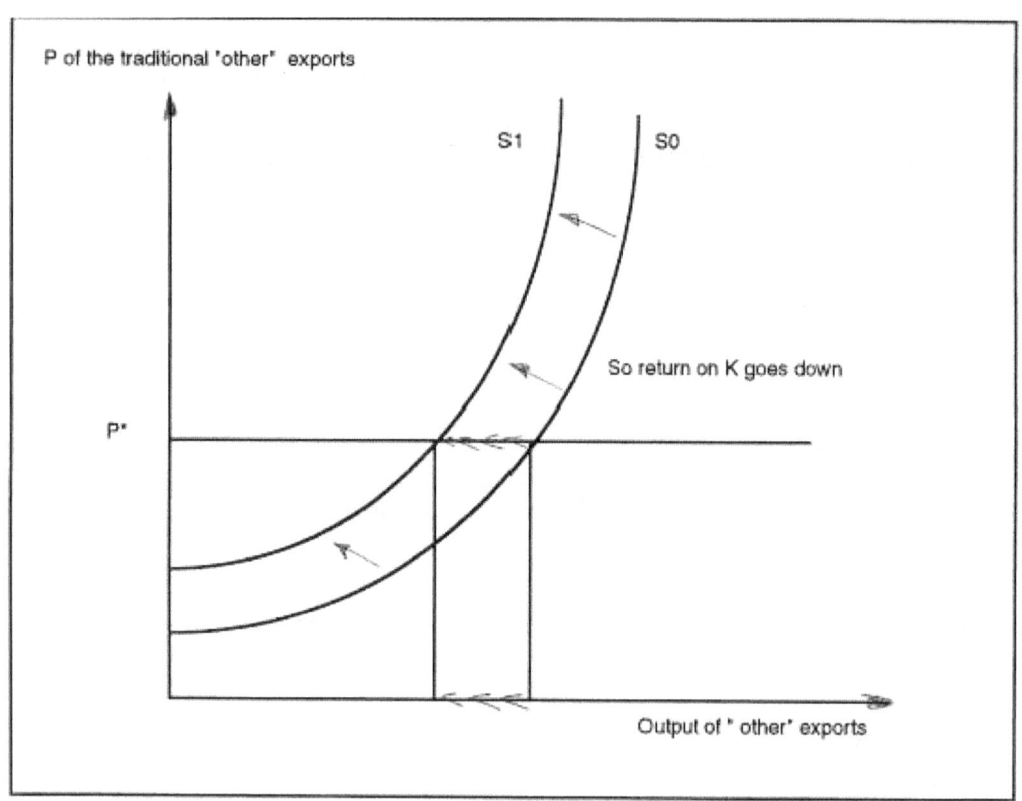

Note: What is very interesting to note here is that there are no problems for the non-traded goods ... **Their prices will go up due to the wage increase!**

F: THE HECKSCHER-OHLIN (ALSO CALLED 2X2X2):

In this chapter, there are four famous results:

I. Rybczinski theorem
II. Stolper-Samuelson theorem
III. Trade pattern among countries
IV. Factor Prices Equalization (FPE)

The assumptions of this famous model are quite stringent, and they have been relaxed here and there in the trade literature. However, in this course, we will stick to the original presentation of the model.

- 2 goods: Food and Clothing
- 2 factors K and L, CRTS
- perfect competition
- full employment
- K and L fixed (or parametric)
- only one w and r

Here, on the graph, food is K-intensive, Clothing is L-intensive [do you really understand WHY?], and A and B are the least cost K/L chosen to produce Food and Clothing for a given wage-rental ratio:

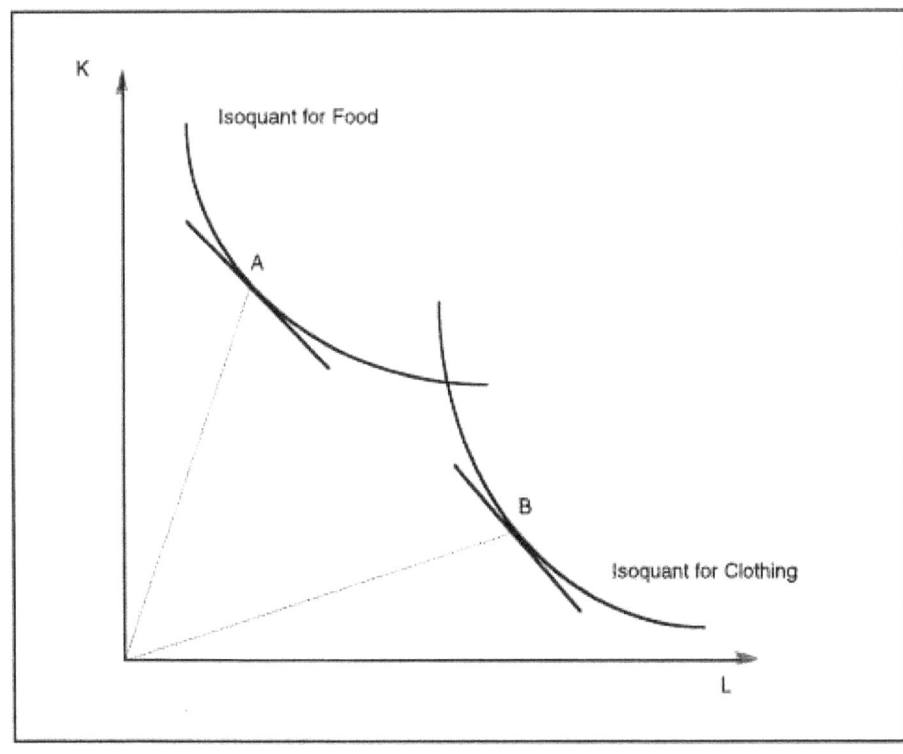

I: The Rybczynski theorem:

What is happening to employment of K and L?

Remember: Full <u>employment</u> ...

$$K=KC+KF$$
$$L=LC+LF$$

so we have:

$$a(lc).Xc + a(lf).Xf = L$$
$$a(kc).Xc + a(kf).Xf = K$$

Again, same idea, full employment means that the supply of factors of production is equal to the demand for these factors. Also, note that these constraints are linear so we can represent them in a two-dimension graph:

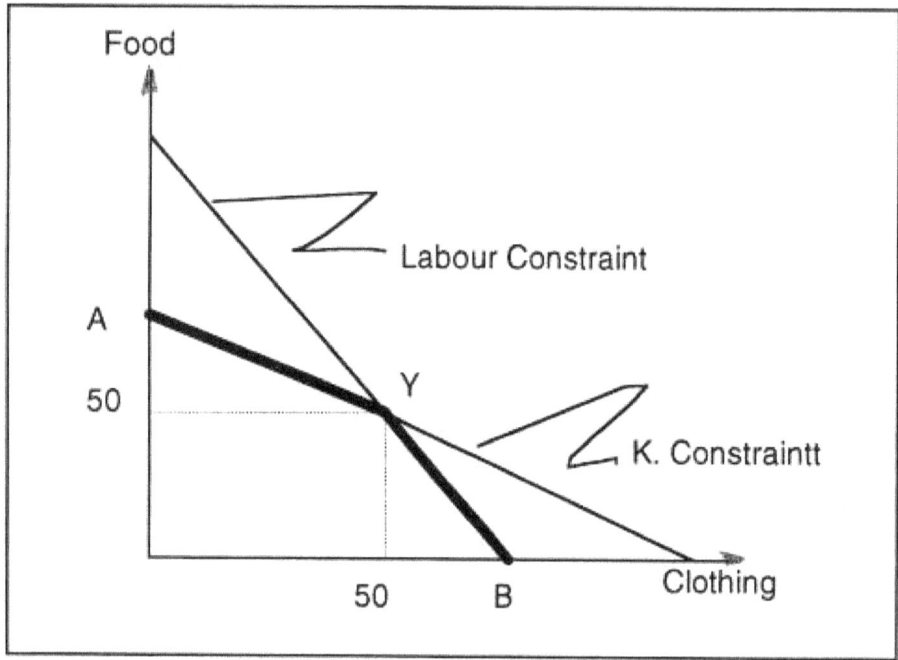

labor constraint = F = 200 - 3.0 [slope = - a(lc)/a(lf)]
capital constraint = F = 100 - C [slope = - a(kc)/a(kf)]

Thick area: where all constraints are met.

Only Y is full employment of both factors.

Along AY, we have full employment of K, but some L are unemployed.

Along BY, we have full employment of L, but some K are unemployed.

Numerical example:
    L = 200 units
    K = 100 units

Suppose that: a(lc) = 3
                 a(lf) = 1
                 a(kc) = 1
                 a(kf) = 1

So the constraints can be expressed as:

    $3 \cdot X_c + 1 \cdot X_f = 200$ [Labour]   (I)
    $1 \cdot X_c + 1 \cdot X_f = 100$ [Capital]   (II)

Solve: $X_f = 100 - X_c$ (from II) and replace in (I):

$3X_c + 100 - X_c = 200$
$2 \cdot X_c = 100$ so $X_c = 50$ and $X_f = 50$

Note: food is capital intensive and clothing is labour intensive because: $a(kf)/a(lf) > a(kc)/a(lc)$

But what happens if one of the endowments is going up?
For instance, labour is increasing, but w/r is the same so techniques won't change.

This can be seen graphically, first:

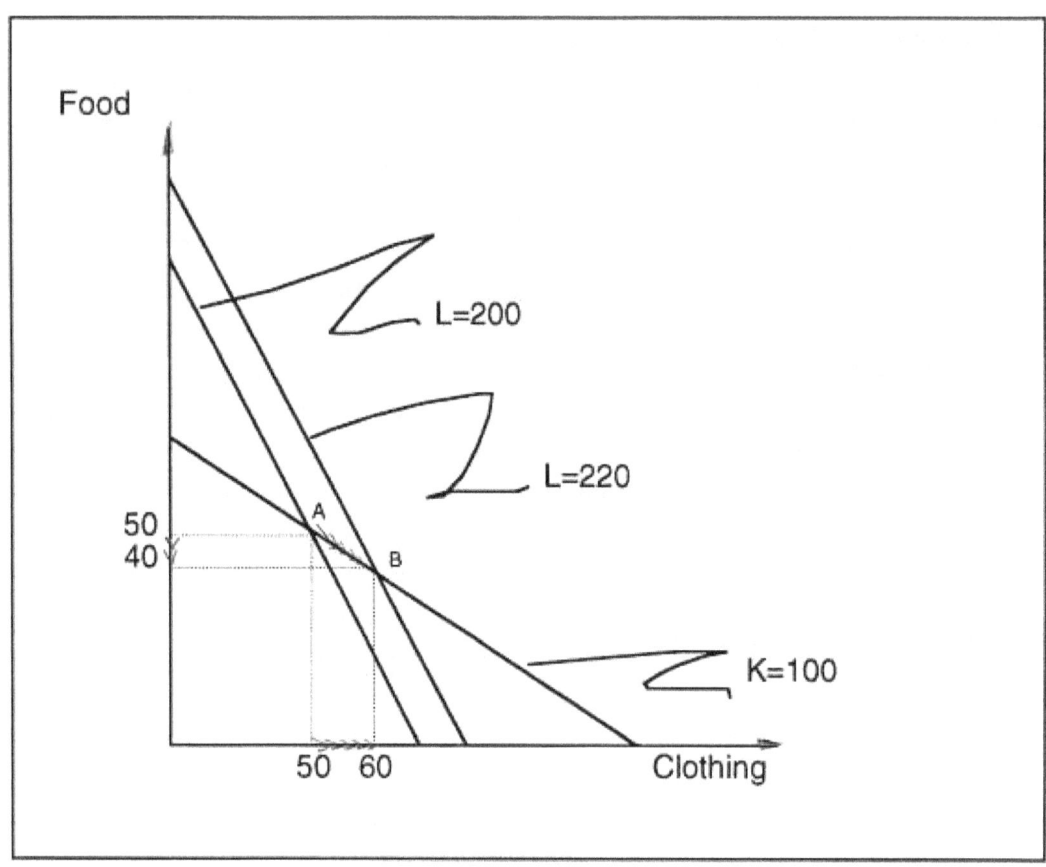

So, if the supply of labor increases (role of immigration, for instance), the production of clothing (the labour intensive good), expands by a magnified amount, while the production of the capital intensive good decreases by a magnified amount .... this is the RYBCZYNSKI theorem. (1st result).

II: The Stolper-Samuelson theorem:

The corollary to this theorem is the STOLPER-SAMUELSON theorem: it answers questions like: what happens if the price of a product goes up/down while the other one stays the same?

For instance, the price of a product could go up as a result of tariff...

The key idea of the Stolper-Samuelson theorem is that the return of the factor that is used intensively in the good whose price is going up, will UNAMBIGUOUSLY increase, while the return on the factor that is used intensively in the good whose price is unchanged will UNAMBIGUOUSLY decrease (2nd result)

So here, let us see what happens when Pc is increased (for instance, because a tariff has been imposed on clothing), and Pf = 0 [remember clothing is labour intensive]. Also, assume that endowments stay the same [what we are doing now is to study one problem at the time].

So suppose a tariff is levied on imported clothing:

Remember, we have competition so that:

a(lc).w + a(kc).r = Pc
a(lf).w + a(kf).r = Pf,

Graphically, we have:

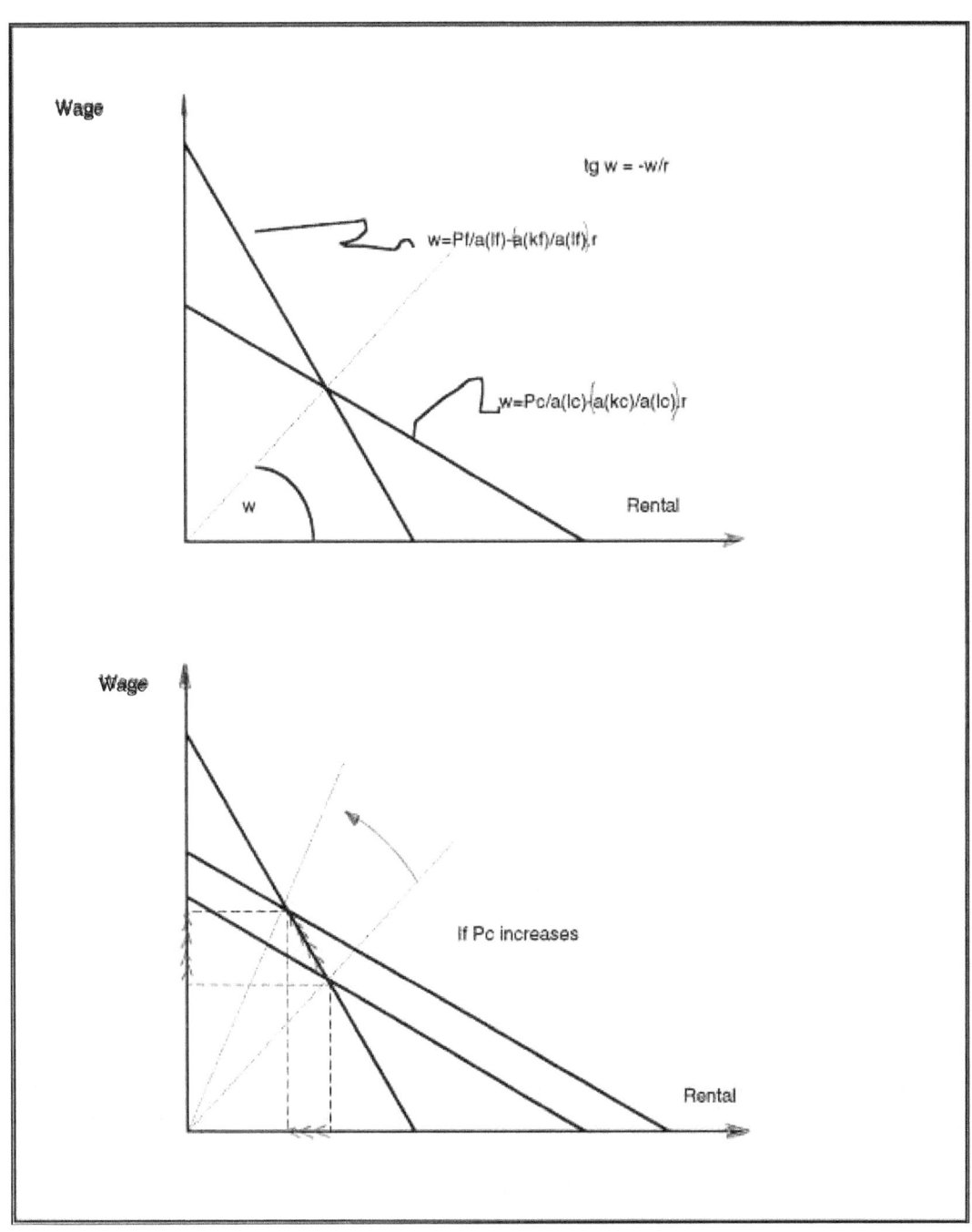

Remember that we have: a(kf)/a(lf) > a(kc)/a(lc) (because, by assumption, food is K intensive and C is labour intensive).

So as Pc increases, we get the following result (no proof is provided here, lack of time):

$w >> P_F > r$

This theorem is crucial because --contrary to the neoclassical ambiguity obtained earlier-- it is possible to show that the government can improve UNAMBIGUOUSLY the fate of one group (workers OR capitalists) by implementing a certain tariff policy.

III: International trade and the H.O. model:

The objective of this paragraph is to derive the last two famous results from the H.O. model: the trade pattern and the factor price equalization.

Let us assume that:
- technology is the same
- tastes are similar.

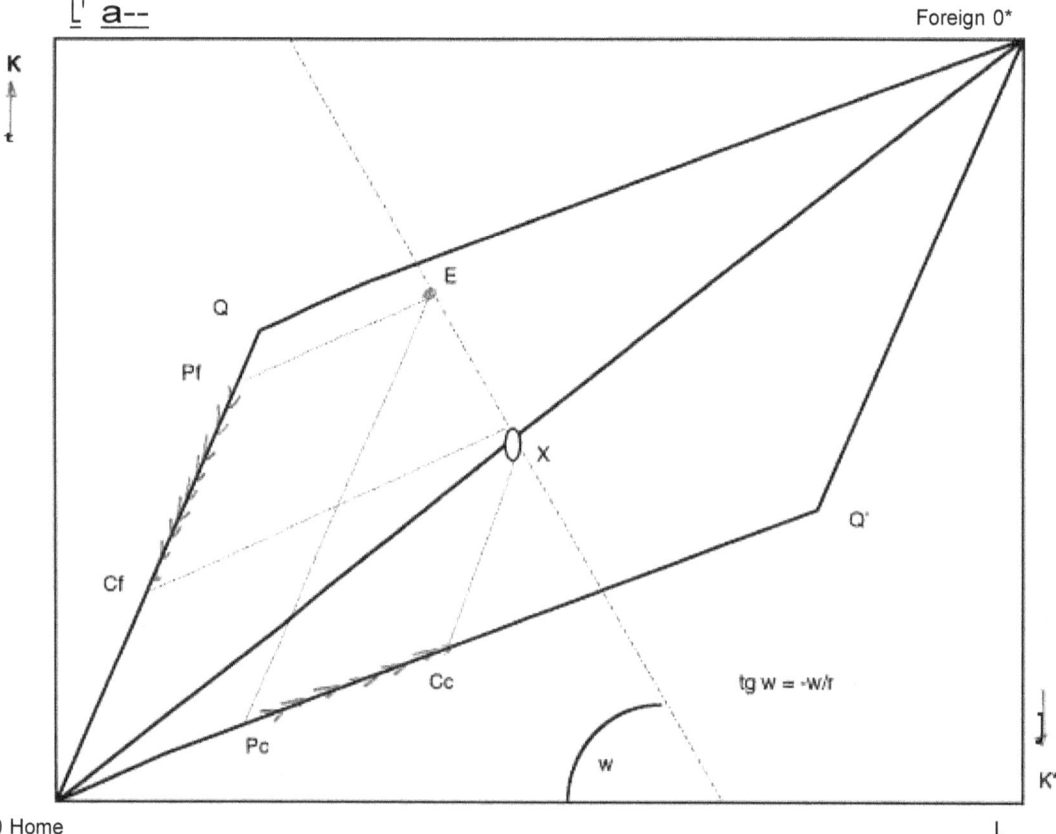

E is initial endowment:

E is above 00*, so home is relatively capital-rich (for instance Canada). And the foreign country is relatively labour-rich (for instance Mexico).

The slope of OQ is the K/L ratio to produce food at home = slope of O*Q' = K/L ratio to produce food abroad. This is the graphical representation of the assumption that the techniques are the same in the two countries.
Similarly, the slope of 0Q' is the K/L ratio to produce clothing at home = slope 0*Q = K/L ratio to produce clothing abroad.

Point X divides the diagonal into 2 segments that are proportional to the countries' GDP levels. This OX/XO* is equal to the relative GDP level in the home country. Now we can choose units of measurement so that:

    0Q = World production of food
    0Q' = World production of clothing

so 00* is the World GDP.

Now you see that home/foreign <u>GDP</u> increases as the wage-rental ratio decreases. This is because --at a given E-- home is relatively K abundant.

Why should W be this or that? In other words, what are the forces that determine the wage-rental ratio?

Role of relative demand. Suppose tastes --remember, for simplicity, tastes are the same in both countries-- are suddenly heavily biased in favour of Food/Clothing, then P_f/P_c increases and the rental goes up while the wage decreases.

<u>For food:</u>

OPF = production of food at home
OCF = consumption of food at home with free trade.

QPF = production of food abroad
QCF = consumption of food abroad

So the home country, the relatively K rich country exports the K intensive good.

CF - PF = our export = their import (of food)

Similarly, <u>for clothing,</u>

OPC = production of clothing at home
OCC = consumption of clothing at home

Q'PC = production of clothing abroad
Q'CC = consumption of clothing abroad

So the foreign country (the relatively labour rich country) exports clothing (the labour intensive good). This is our third result: in the H.O model, Theorem III is that trade patterns are a function of the **RELATIVE** abundance of factors of production.

Now pushing the case to the extreme, we can say that --because we have assumed that tastes, techniques were the same-- if two countries have the same K/L ratio before trade, they will not gain by opening to free trade! This is because if they have the same "everything" in autarky, they will have the same autarky relative price and so will have no incentive to engage in trade. (cf. our first models at the beginning of this course).

Why do we have factor price equalization? Let us look at the graph again: By exporting the K intensive good, it is just like exporting K itself so r (the return on capital) will increase until $r/w = r^*/w^*$, then at the limit relative costs become the same so relative prices become the same - no need to do additional trade! - FPE. (4th result)

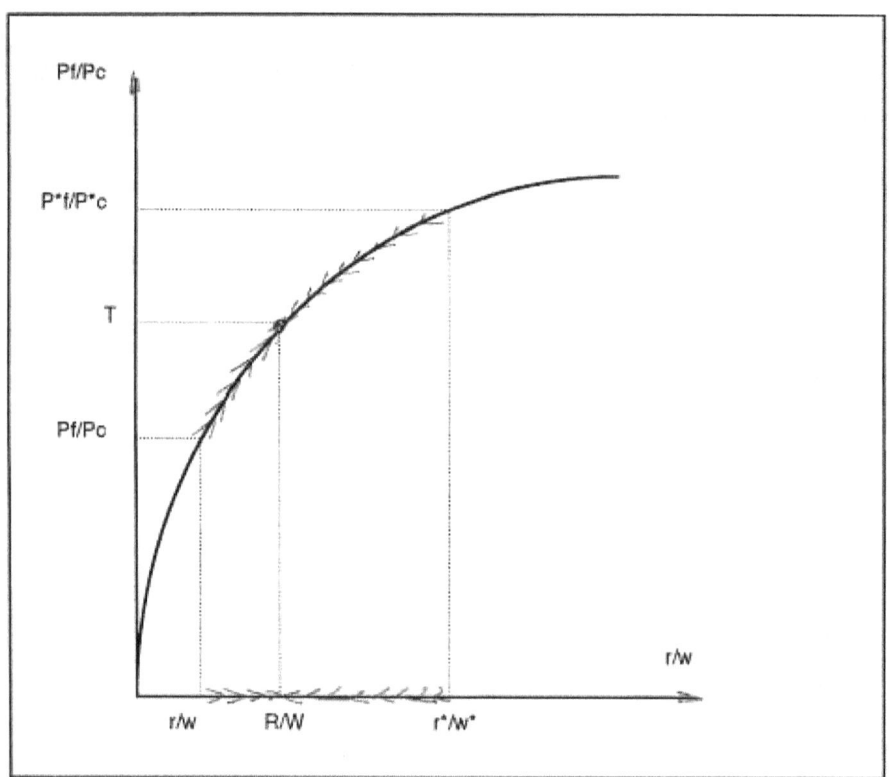

This equality arises because the 2 countries share the same technology and have the same tastes. So in equilibrium we have... with free trade:

$w \cdot a(lc) + r \cdot a(kc) = Pc$ = world price of clothing

$w^* \cdot a(lc) + r^* \cdot a(kc) = Pc =$ "

$w \cdot a(lf) + r \cdot a(kc) = Pf$ = world price of food

$w^* \cdot a(lf) + r^* \cdot a(kf) = Pf = $ "   "

Empirical tests of this model: The Leontief Paradox:

US should --as a K intensive country-- exports K intensive goods and imports L intensive goods. Leontief (a famous economist) calculated the amount of K and L necessary to produce 1 m $ worth of US exports and 1 m $ worth of US goods competing with US imports.

He expected that the exports would require more K/L than the import-competing goods... But, in fact, he found that import-competing goods required 30% more K per labour than the US exports! (which is the exact opposite of what was predicted by the H.O. model).

Economists were very upset!

So they tried to explain:

I. May be L US is different from the L ABROAD (for instance L US would be so productive ... 3 times --so US would be a L rich country).

II. May be there is a lot of skilled labour/few unskilled labour...
Role of human capital --US capital is also in education...

III. Research & Dev. --because US does a lot of R & D, it exports goods requiring lot of skilled labour...

IV. Natural resource: (our 3rd factor of production). Because the US imports a lot of raw material requiring a lot of K/L - might explain...

V. Tariffs (at various rates) --might disturb the comparison.

VI. Tastes: if as we have seen tastes are different in the US than abroad... might explain trade...

VI. Factor intensity reversal: if food production is K intensive in a K intensive country and L intensive in a L rich country (compared to other goods)...

Now empirical researches are made by econometricians. For instance, E. Leamer (from the UCLA) says that the H.O. model is valid empirically after all.

To prove his point, he took many countries at the time: "A country endowed with a relatively large proportion of the world's stock of a factor of production should make large net exports of products intensive in that factor."

Trend: The works by P. Krugman (from the MIT): he introduces imperfect competition in HOS. And, from his researches, it is then possible to justify that, under very special circumstances, pure free trade might not be optimum for a country.

G: TARIFFS AND OTHER ASPECTS OF PROTECTION THEORY:

Today, optimum tariffs are one of the hottest subject in trade theory: people now study the opportunity of imposing import -subsidies! (i.e. negative tariff).

Tariff analysis is very different according to the size of the country:

We will distinguish the two traditional cases: **the small country case** and **the large country case.**

First case: assume a small country:

Here a small country means that world prices are fixed for this country [this is the neoclassical version of "small country"]. In other words, a small country can not --by its actions concerning supply and demand-- influence the price of goods.

A tariff is a tax on the importation of a commodity from abroad.
A tariff t will reduce imports and attract resources into the protected sector.

With a tariff, t (a rate), $P_f = (1 + t) \cdot P_f^*$ = price of food at home [if food is the imported commodity].

A tariff changes the relative P_c/P_t at home while leaving the relative world price P_c^*/P_f^* unchanged.

This can be seen graphically for by concentrating:

    [I] on production,
    [II] on demand,
    [III] **on imports.**

[I] What about production?

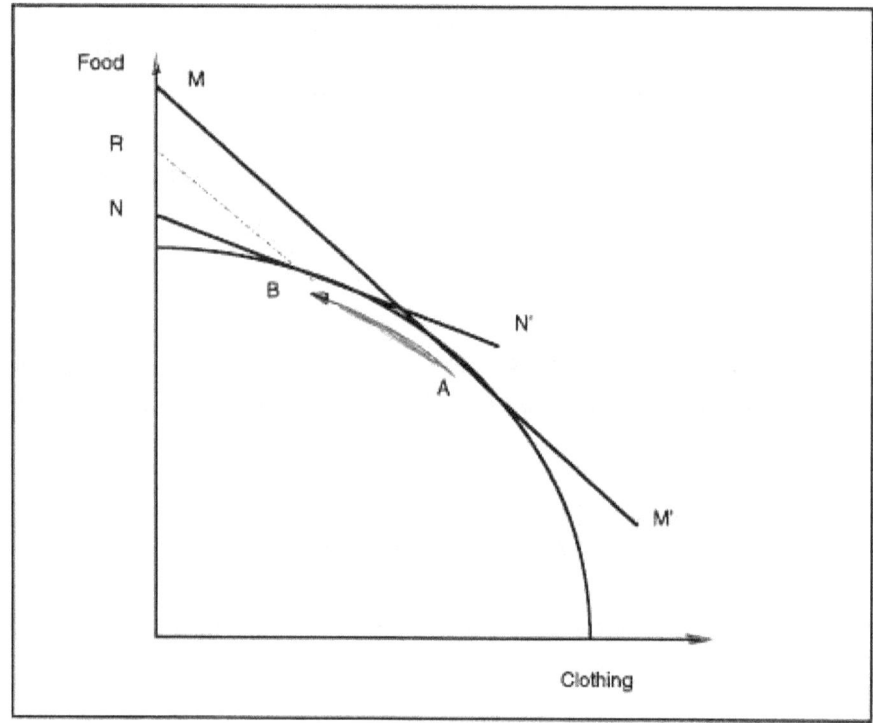

Comments: initially - no tariffs - we produce at A and Pc/Pf is given at MM'.

Now the GVT imposes a tariff on imported food, so the relative price paid by the consumer becomes slope NN'

Productive resources are attracted by this new relative price and they leave the clothing industry and move to the food industry: production moves along the PPF from A to B.

At world prices, the national income measured in food units has decreased from M to R.

[II]: But what about demand?

To study demand, let us assume that production stays the same [so we can study _only_ the demand side of the problem].

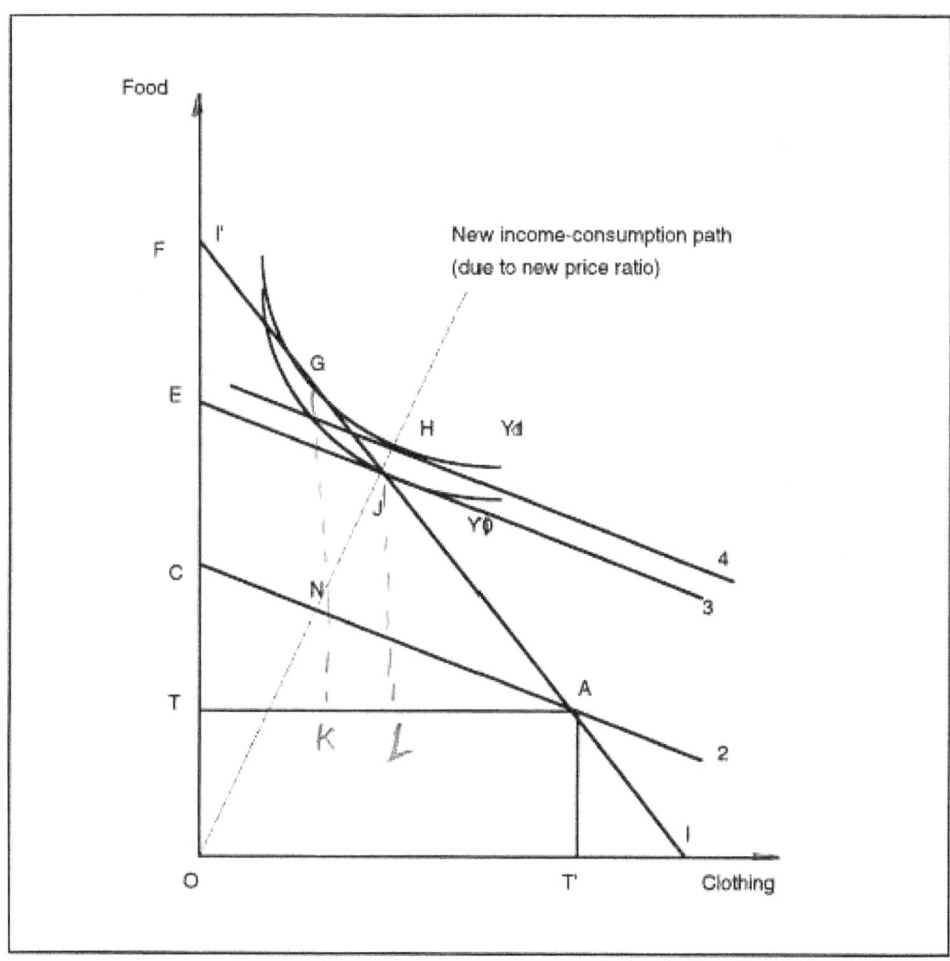

Assumptions and comments for this graph:

i) TAT[1] is our PPF (so before and after tariff, production stays at A). This is done to simplify the analysis and concentrate our attention on the demand side of the problem. Price ratio is slope of line II'(in absolute value).

ii) The utility function is "homothethique" (MRS is constant along the income-consumption line) and any other ray starting through the origin. Again, this assumption is more for the elegance of the graph and will not influence the kind of results we will get.

iii) Initially, we produce at A (this is obvious because we assume full employment and point A is the only one on the PPF that will allow to have that full employment), consume at G (before the tariff) and reach the level of utility or level of income YO. The trade triangle is GKA.

iv) The government decides to impose a tariff on the imported good (= food), but will give back the revenue of the tariff to the consumers.

v) So <u>at home,</u> the relative price <u>Pc/Pf</u> is now equal to the slope (in absolute value) of the line 2 or 3 or 4.

vi) The movement from G to H represents the substitution effect. Indeed, at H, we are on the same indifference curve as before, but with the new price ratio. But we can not stay at H. Why? Because at H the value --at world prices-- of our consumption would be higher than the value of our production.

vii) So we must go at J because J is on the income consumption line ONCE (this is to satisfy our requirement of homotheticity) <u>and,</u> at J, the world value of our production = world value of consumption (this is balanced trade). So, the new trade triangle with the Rest of the World is JLA. Note that trade has shrunk as a result of the imposition of the tariff, and this does not even take the possible retaliation from the Rest of the World into consideration

viii) The distance EC measures the tariff revenue in food units... Why?
Home value of production is OC --but home disposable income is OE ... So the difference is brought by the tariff revenue.

[III] What about imports?

How do they change as a result of the imposition of a tariff? Let us combine the first two graphs, ...

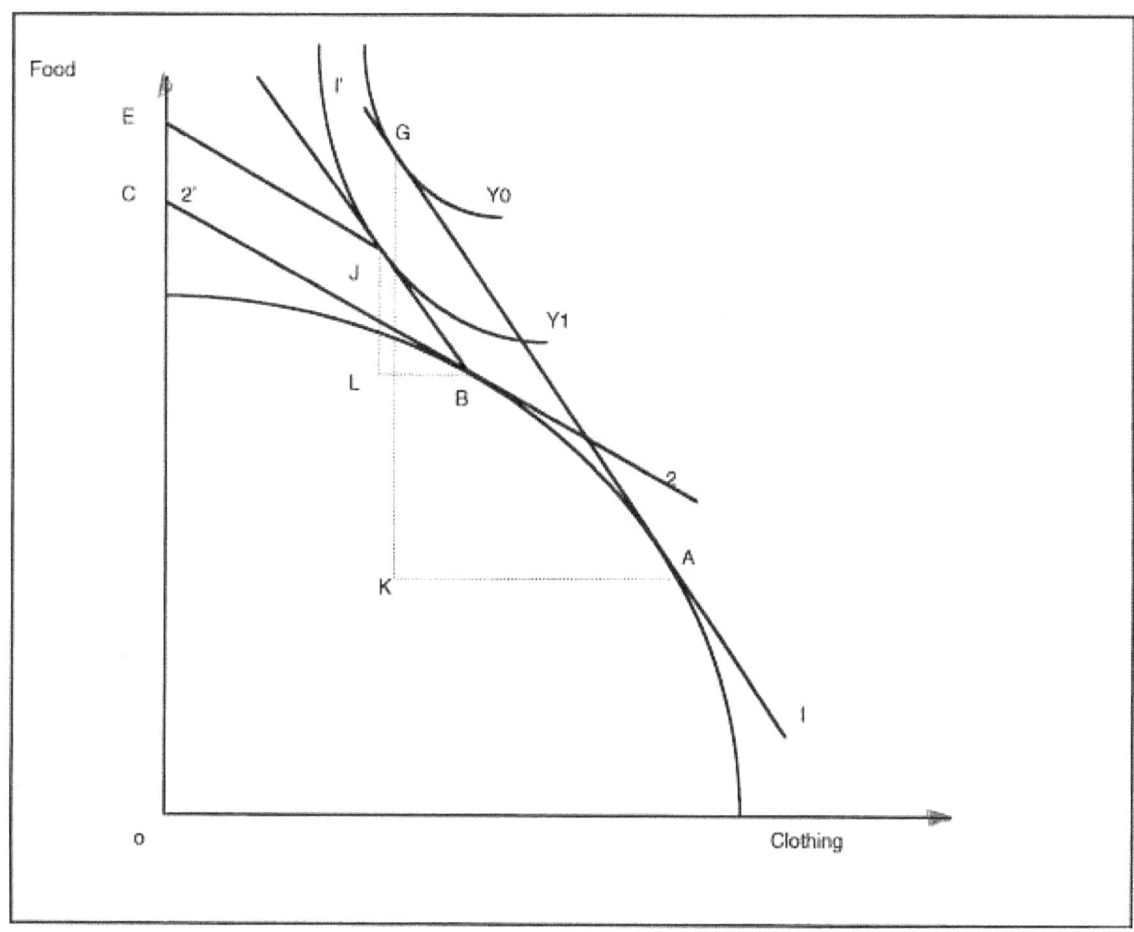

At the beginning, we produce at A and consume at G, so trade triangle is GAK.

Tariff is imposed so new relative price at home is slope of 2 (in absolute value). Now production is at B and new consumption is at J and so the new trade triangle is at JLB.

Disposable income = tariff revenue + home value of production
   OE   =   EC   +   OC

Note that the home production of imports - competing goods (food at home) is going up.

Conclusions of the tariff analysis on a small country:

For a small country (one that can NOT influence relative world prices), the imposition of a tariff has 5 consequences:

(i)   it lowers welfare (from Y0 to Y1)

ii)   it creates a tariff revenue

(iii) it increases the production of import-competing goods

(iv) it reduces imports

(v)   it shrinks the trade triangle - volume of international trade is going down.

Note: export tax:

There are 2 historical examples that come to mind:

a- Long time ago, some countries wanted to limit the exports of the commodities they thought were essential [for instance France (mercantilist)/coal...) to make war...]. So they imposed a tax on exports... and to boot, they collected the revenue...

b- Today, imposing an export tax is a preventive move. Famous example: Canada has a very special way of allocating rights to cut lumber (cf. B.C.). So sometimes they are very competitive in the U.S. markets. The U.S. lumber industry complained and the U.S. government threatened Canada with a tariff if Canada did not change its way... so Canada imposed an export tariff --pleased US and collected revenue itself.

Second case: assume a large country:

So far we have seen the case of small countries. May be it is more interesting to study large countries: "If the tariff-levying country is not small in relation to world markets, its tariff will drive down the world relative price of imports or equivalently raise the relative world price of its exports. The tariff can improve the country's terms of trade!"

Graphically,

Suppose a country imports food and exports clothing.

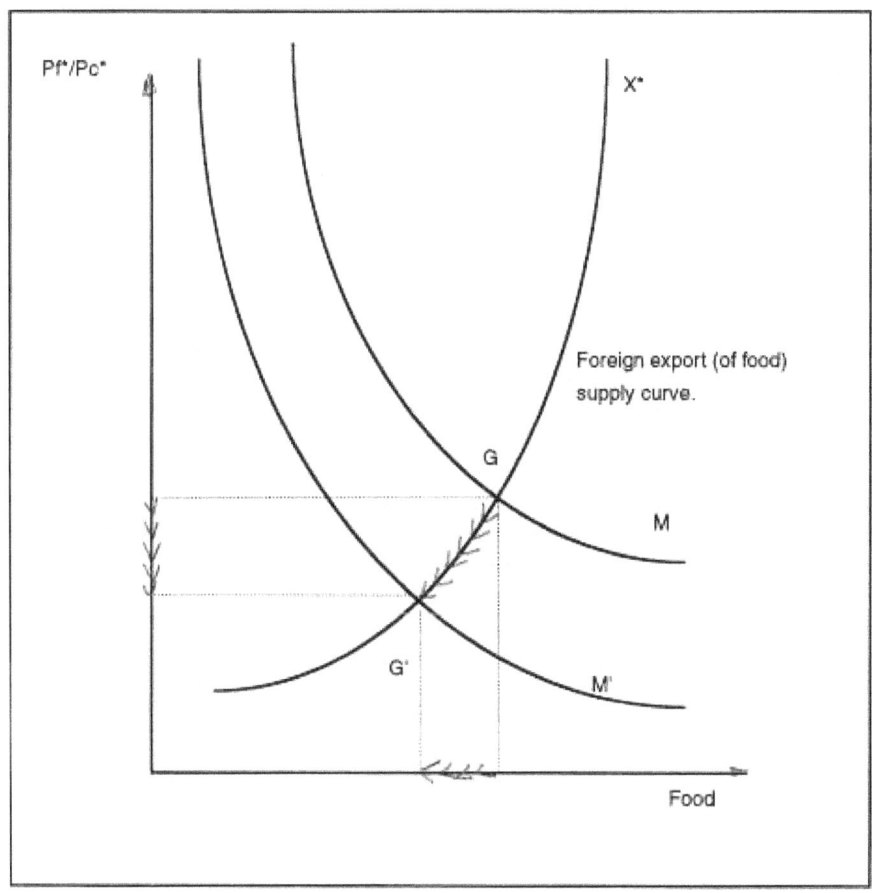

M = our demand for imported food
Ml = our demand for imported food with tariff.

The new relative price of food on the world market is lower than before, our terms of trade have improved!

Now Pf* + tariff = food price at home.

But if P_f^*/P_c^* drops so much ... it is possible that the new domestic price with tariff is lower than the old domestic price without tariff. This is like having your cake and eating it too! In economics, it is called the Metzler paradox.

Note: when a small country imposes a tariff on food, the terms of trade remain unchanged. This is because a small country can not influence the world relative price:

Graphically, the preceding graph is now transformed into a simpler one: the home country can vary its demand for the imported good (food), but it won't change the price!

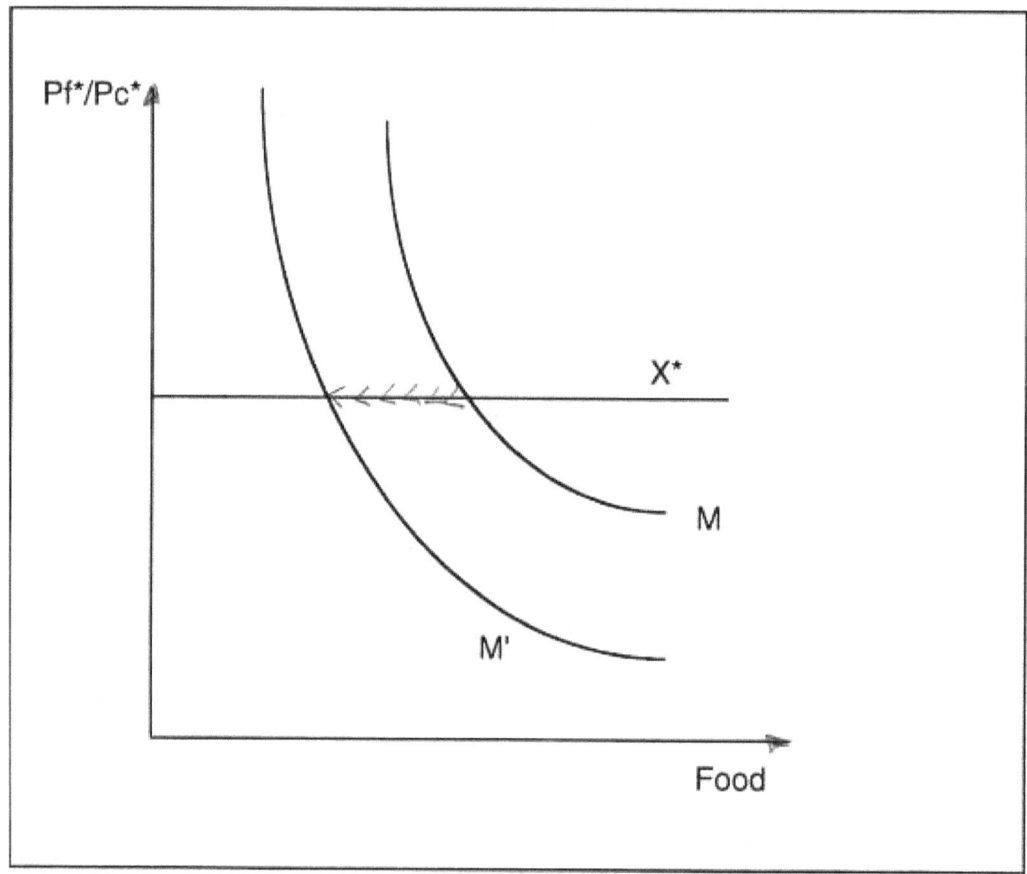

So if a country can influence terms of trade by levying a tariff, then the optimal tariff rate --defined in this course as the one that maximizes income-- might be > 0!

But for a small country, the optimum tariff is always equal to 0.

Graphically, we have:

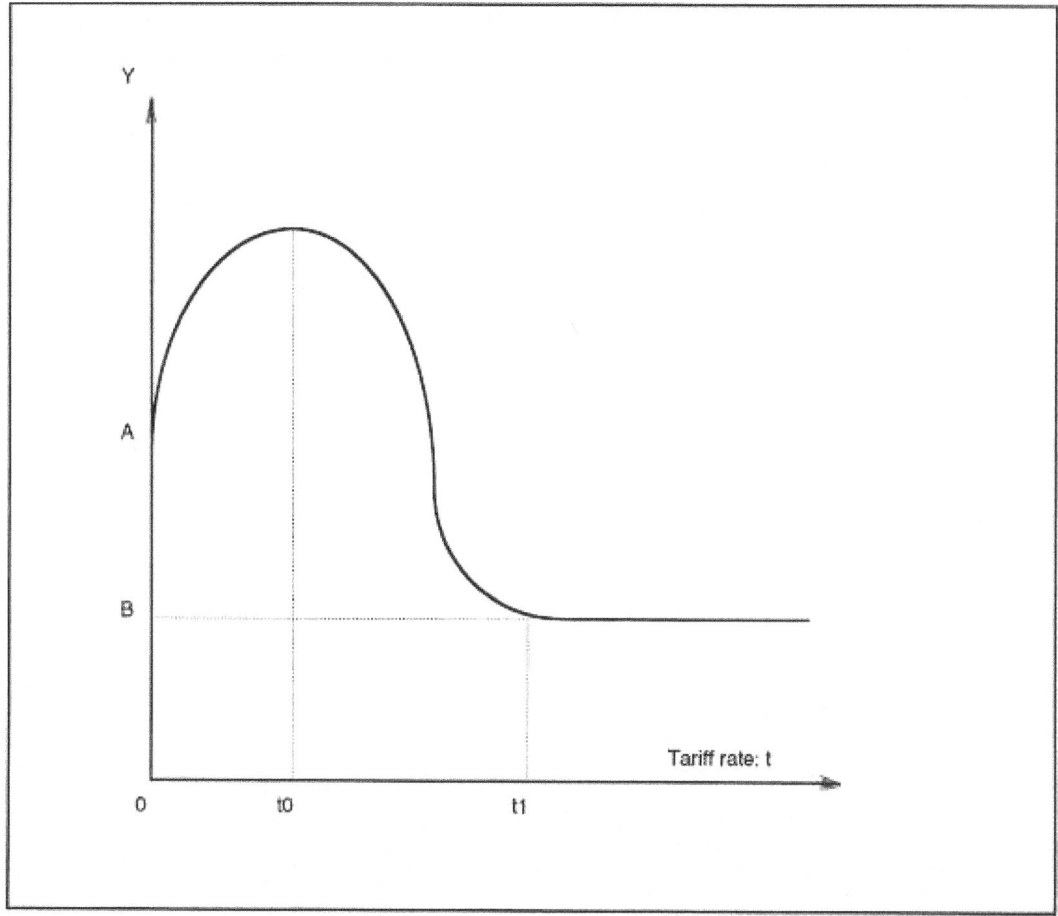

Comment: at 0, there is no more trade, so YA is greater than YB.

For a large country, introducing a tariff is a negative sum game: if you win something, others will lose more [cf. distortion].

Let us examine that statement (which in fact is a justification for the efforts to abolish tariff around the world --GATT) from two points of view: **the production and the consumption:**

Firstly, the production aspect:

Suppose a world, where the home country imports food and exports clothing, but also has imposed a tariff on food.

The following graph shows the situation with tariff and that if removed, we would increase world production.

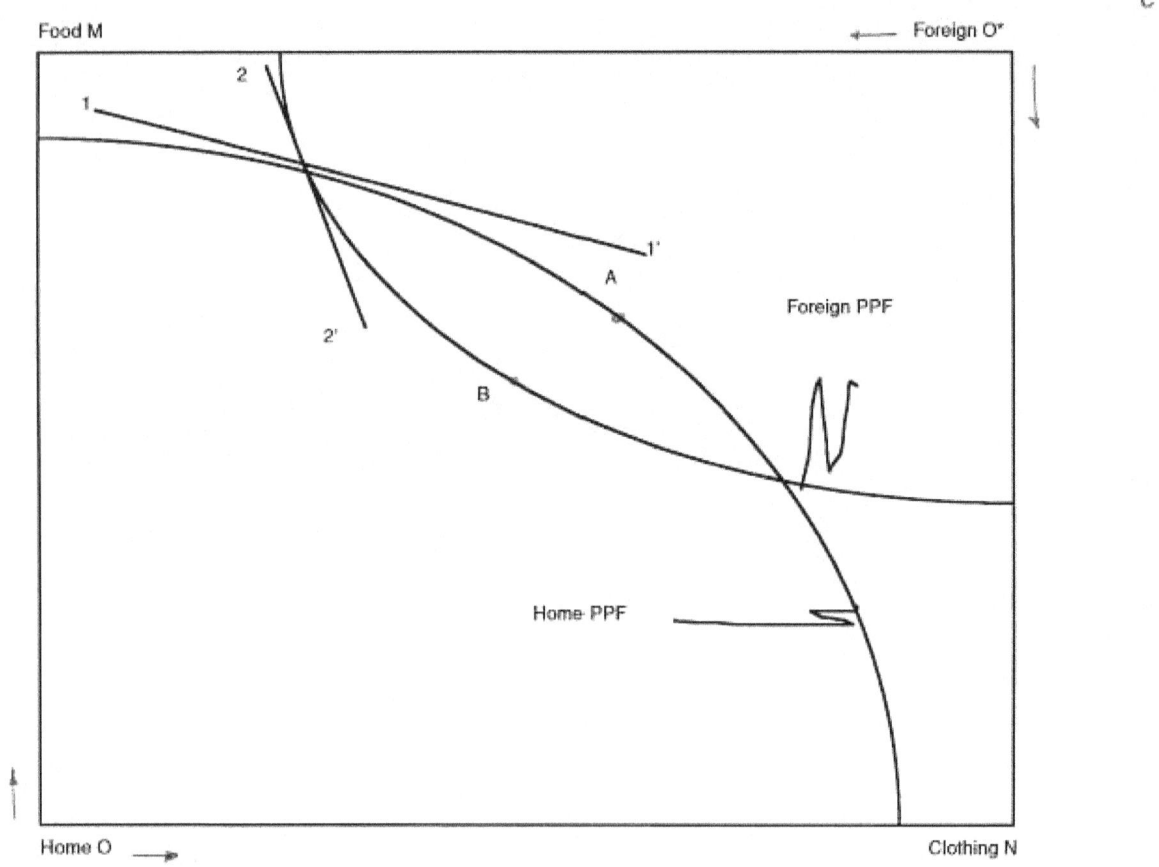

With the tariff on food, Pf/Pc at home > Pf/Pc abroad, this is why, in absolute value, the slope of 1 1' is flatter than the slope of 2 2'.

So (world) total output is OM of food and ON of clothing. But if tariff is removed, there will be one relative price, so HOME COUNTRY will produce more clothing and less food at A and foreign country will produce more food and less clothing at B. And we have: A + B = C. So the world gains from the removal of tariff.

Secondly, the consumption aspect:

Now, we are working with --community-- indifference curves:

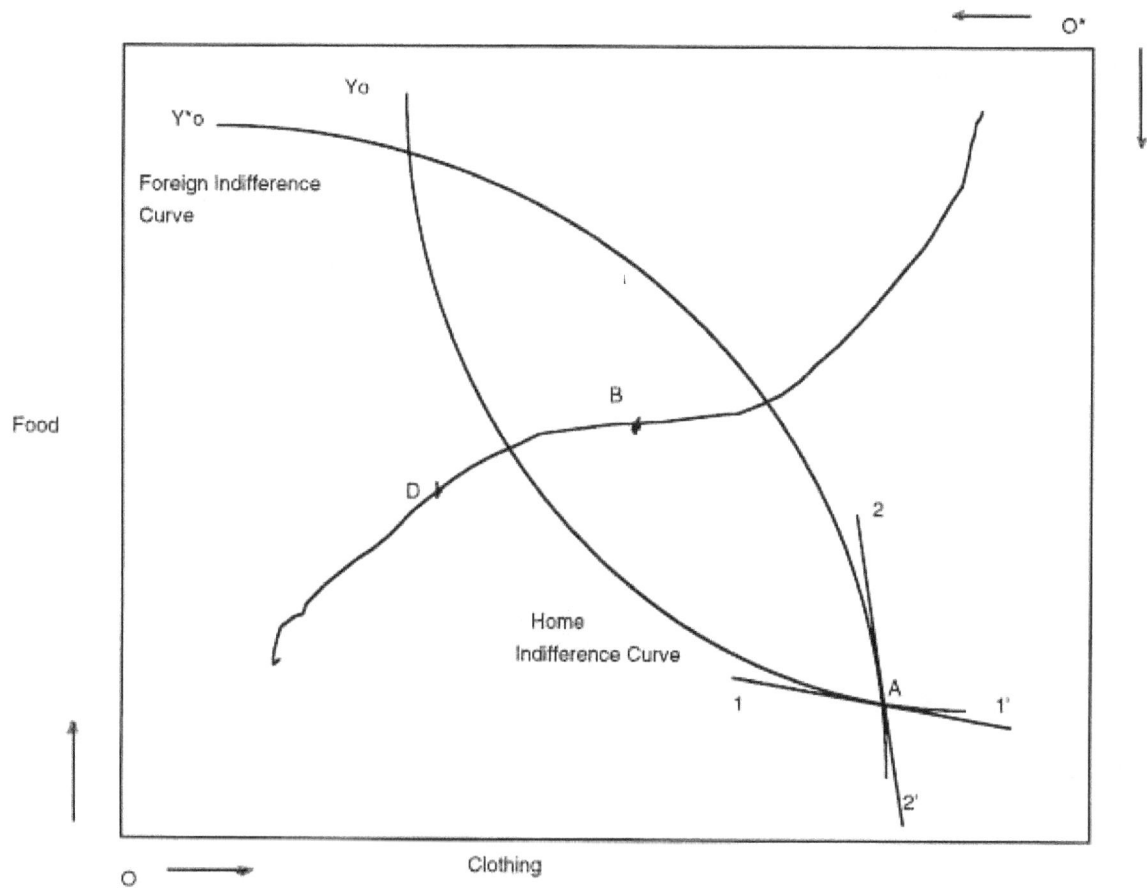

Comments:

Suppose we start at D on the contract curve. No tariff. Now, if a tariff is imposed by the home country in such a way that it improves home welfare (at Yo) and reduces the foreign country's welfare at Yo* --we move from D to A. And we can say that world welfare is reduced in that both country would be better off at B than at A...

The political economy of protection:

Please read very carefully the first paragraph p. 237. It conveys the general philosophy of modern trade theorists who are not too confident with strategic trade policy.

Tariffs are sometimes in fact first a way to collect revenues.
This is a way that pleases the home producers of imports-competing goods, also note that is a very hidden way to get additional revenues and this is often done in LDC's and "planed" economies.

Graphically, the link between an optimum tariff (the one that maximize Y) and the tariff that maximizes tariff revenue (T) is:

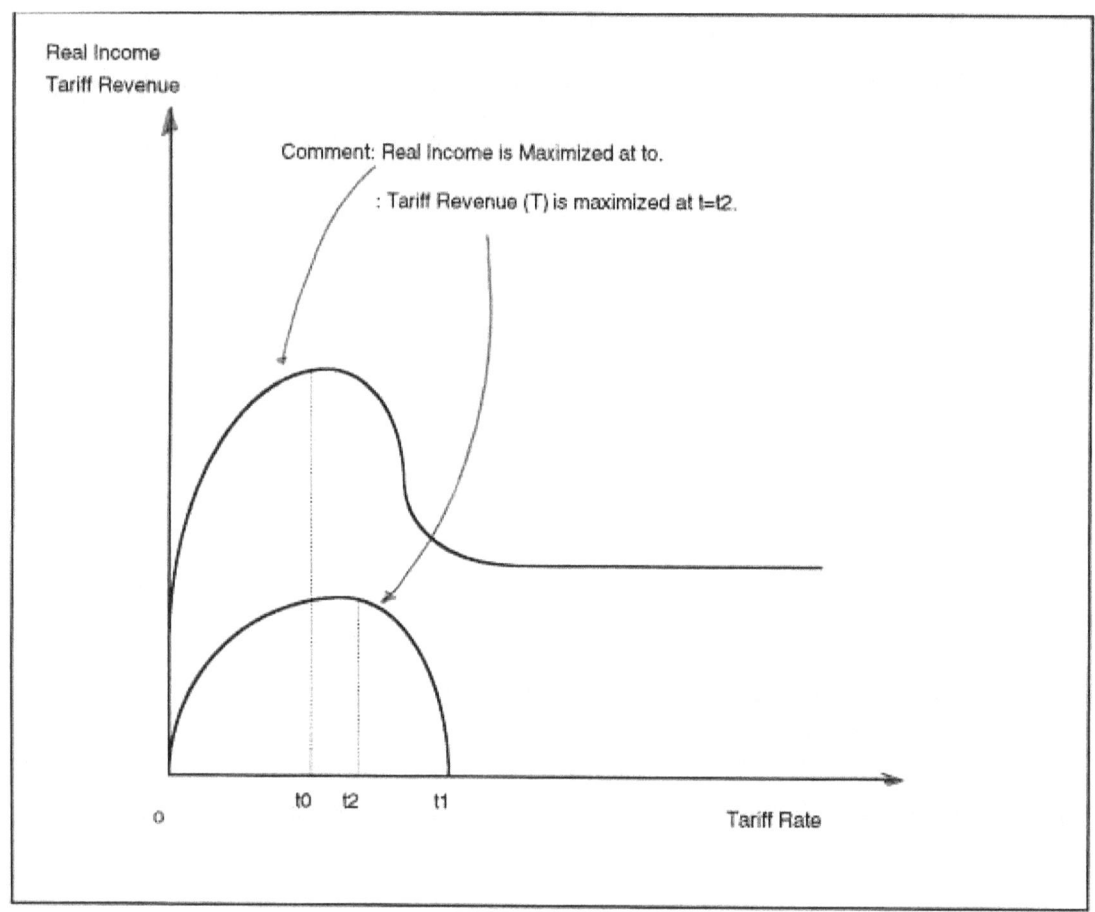

Comment: Real Income is Maximized at t0.
: Tariff Revenue (T) is maximized at t=t2.

Let us prove the key notion that optimal tariff is less than tariff that maximize tariff revenue (T):   t0 < t2

Basic idea of the proof (graphic only): suppose we are at t2, any - very small - additional increase in tariff should let <u>tariff revenue</u> (T) unchanged:

$dT/dt = 0$ (when t is in the neighbourhood of t2), but at the same time: $dY/dt < 0$ (when t is in the neighbourhood of t2).

Graphically,

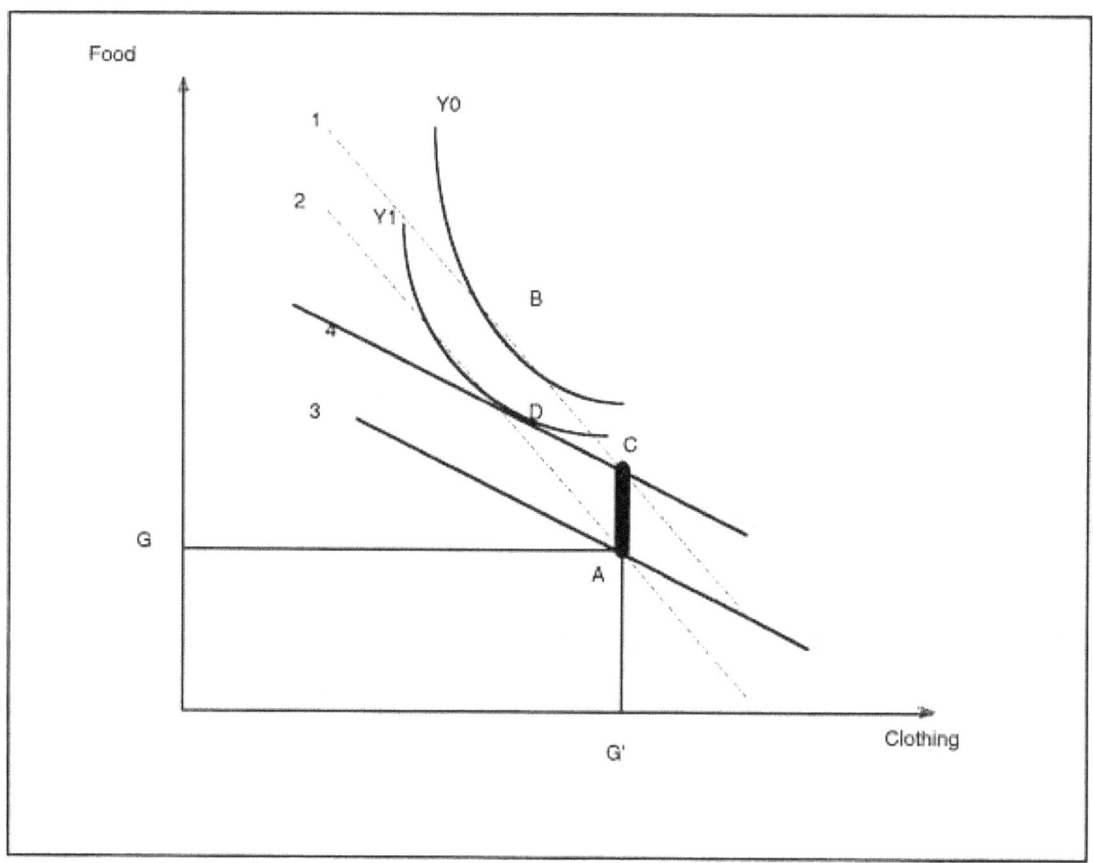

Comments:

- Suppose our PPF is GAG'

- we produce at A, consume at B, slope of 1 or 2 is Pc/Pf at home

- tariff revenue is at its maximum at CA

Now suppose we have a small increase in tariff but because we are at the tariff-maximizing rate, there will be no change in the tariff revenue:

$dT/dt = 0$ (in the neighbourhood of t2)

But as we can see that income drops: from Yo to Y1, we move from B to D in terms of consumption.

The new Pc/Pf is the absolute value of the slope of 3 or 4.

The tariff revenue stays constant and maximum at CA.

Rent-seeking, distribution of income & tariffs

Public choice: applying economics to study politics

- G. Tullock: the "father of modern public choice".

- A. O. Krueger - "The Political Economy of the Rent Seeking Society" (AER, 1974)

- J. N. Bhagwati - "Directly Productive Profit-Seeking Activities" (JPE 82)

- M. Olson - "The logic of collective action" (Harvard University Press, 1965).

Applying public choice theories here leads to two kinds of predictions:

A. You can expect lots of lobbying where the specific factor model seems adequate to represent the economic situation. The specific factor might be hurt. But labour not too much (trapped in between --cf. neoclassical ambiguity).

B. Now, if you use the HOS, then labour (in general) might want to mobilize (cf. STOLPER SAMUELSON theorem).

So very often we have a competition between lobbying groups --the result is that it dissipates the rent. So totally unproductive activities are consuming scarce resources (capital and labour) ...
The only way to avoid that is to limit the power of the State to impose tariffs ... (of course, this proposition, in itself, is controversial).

Let us take an example to illustrate the waste generated by the rent-seeking activities (that is NOT in your book!):

1. Suppose we start at PPF1, in autarky:

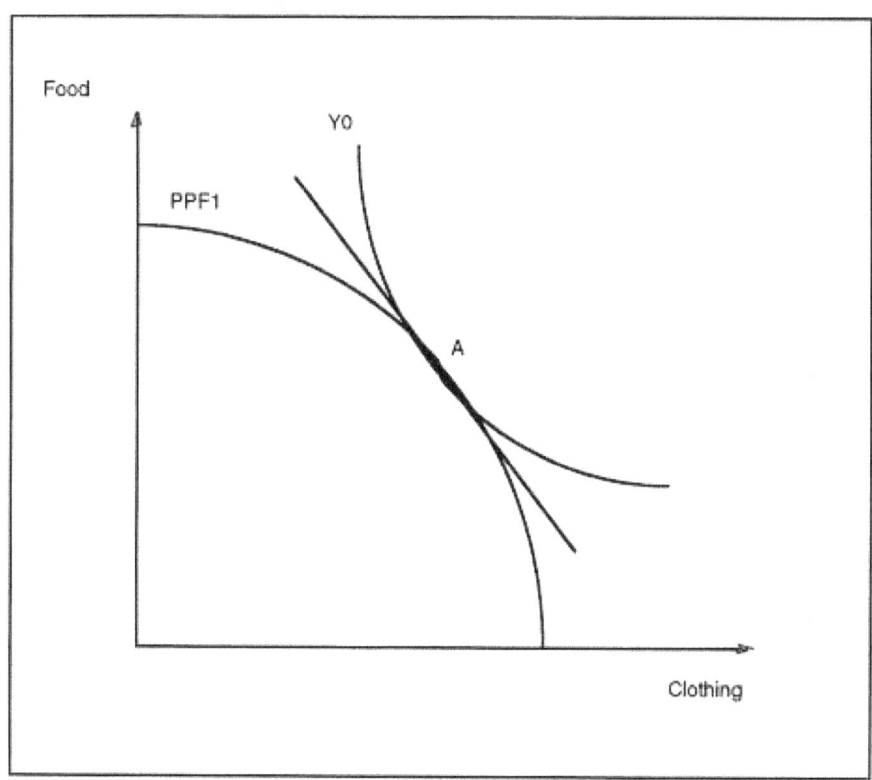

2. Some people want free trade with Rest of the World... And some other groups oppose it. So they fight and spend production resources on that issue ... (cf. Canada).

So we move away form PPF1 to PPF2:

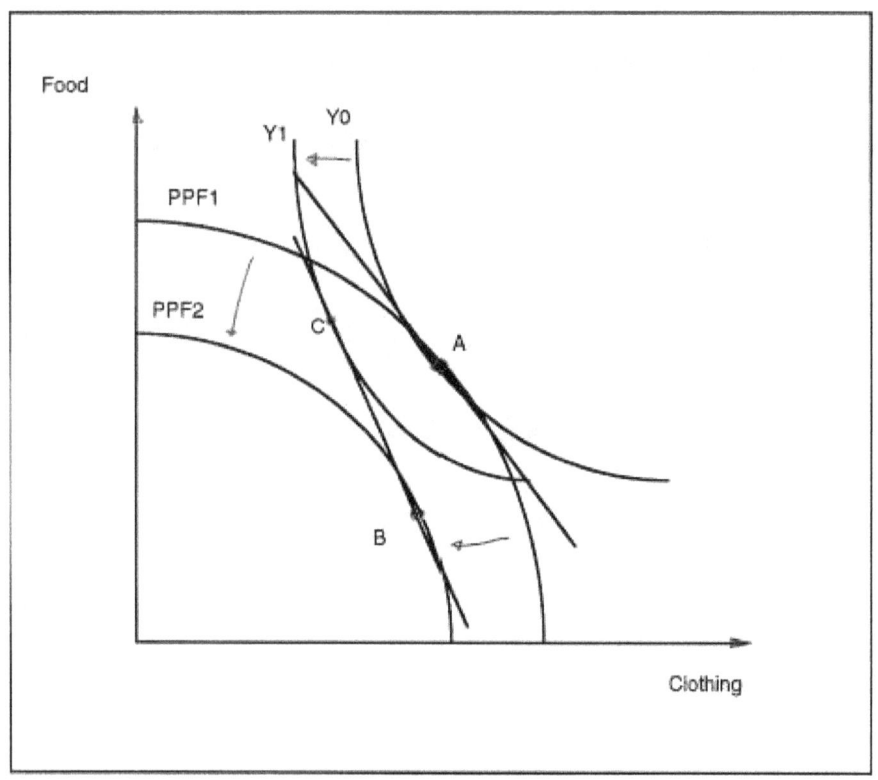

3. Finally, you produce at B (on the PPF2), consume at C. But the utility level is lower than in autarky.

If you think, general equilibrium is relevant, then the attitude towards tariffs is that whatever the goal you are trying to achieve with it (in terms of production - favoring one local industry - or in terms of consumption - favoring the consumption of a certain basket of goods), tariff is quite inefficient to achieve them - there are simpler and better ways to do it.

"Employing tariffs to attain a consumption goal or a production goal is like performing acupuncture with a fork."

. production: subsidy is less damaging than a tariff.
. consumption: tax is less damaging than a tariff.

A tax affects consumption, but leaves producers facing competition at world prices. (i.e. no reallocation of resources...)

Trade creation and trade diversion:

Please read also pp 317 to 321.

This is a very famous concept (Jacob Viner, 1950). Relevant for Canada/US Free Trade deal.

Suppose Country XXX and Country ZZZ form a custom union (this is: eliminate tariffs among themselves and impose a common tariff against the Rest of the World --the custom union is more than a simple free trade deal where each country can keep its own external tariffs).

1st case: Trade creation:

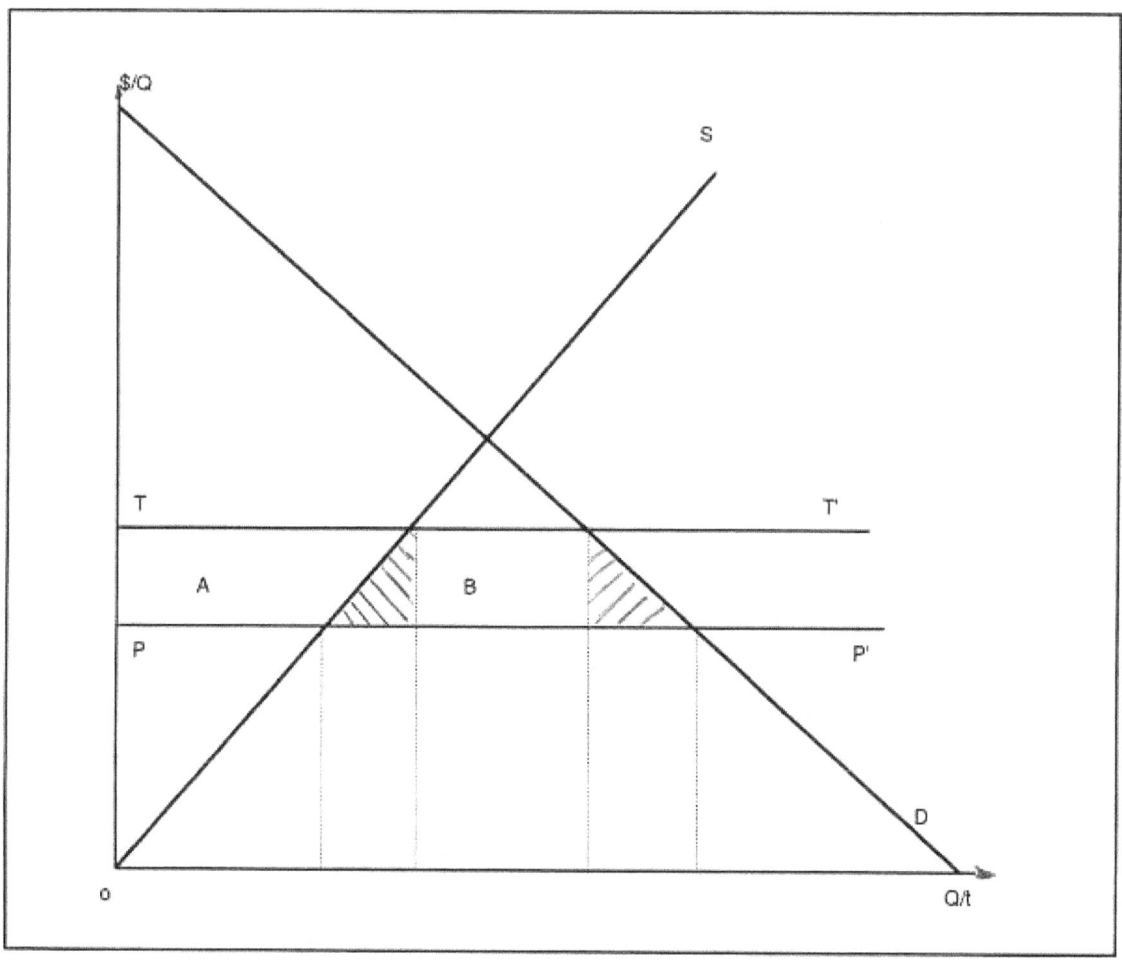

There is a trade creation between countries XXX and ZZZ

"///" and "\\\" = welfare gain due to trade creation.

A = was for home producer, now part of the home consumer surplus
B = was for the State, now part of consumer surplus

2nd case: Trade creation and Trade diversion:

Trade diversion involves a third country: Suppose Japan is the most efficient producer of TV --even more efficient than the US (Country ZZZ).

So Canada, Country XXX, in the absence of any tariff, would consume Japanese TV's (because, on the graph below, Pb > Pc). Now, suppose Canada imposes a tariff (ad valorem) on TV imported. So Canada still consumes Japanese TV's (because, on the graph below, Tb > Tc).

But if Canada and US have now a custom union, the tariff on US made TV's disappears, so Canadian start consuming US made TV's:

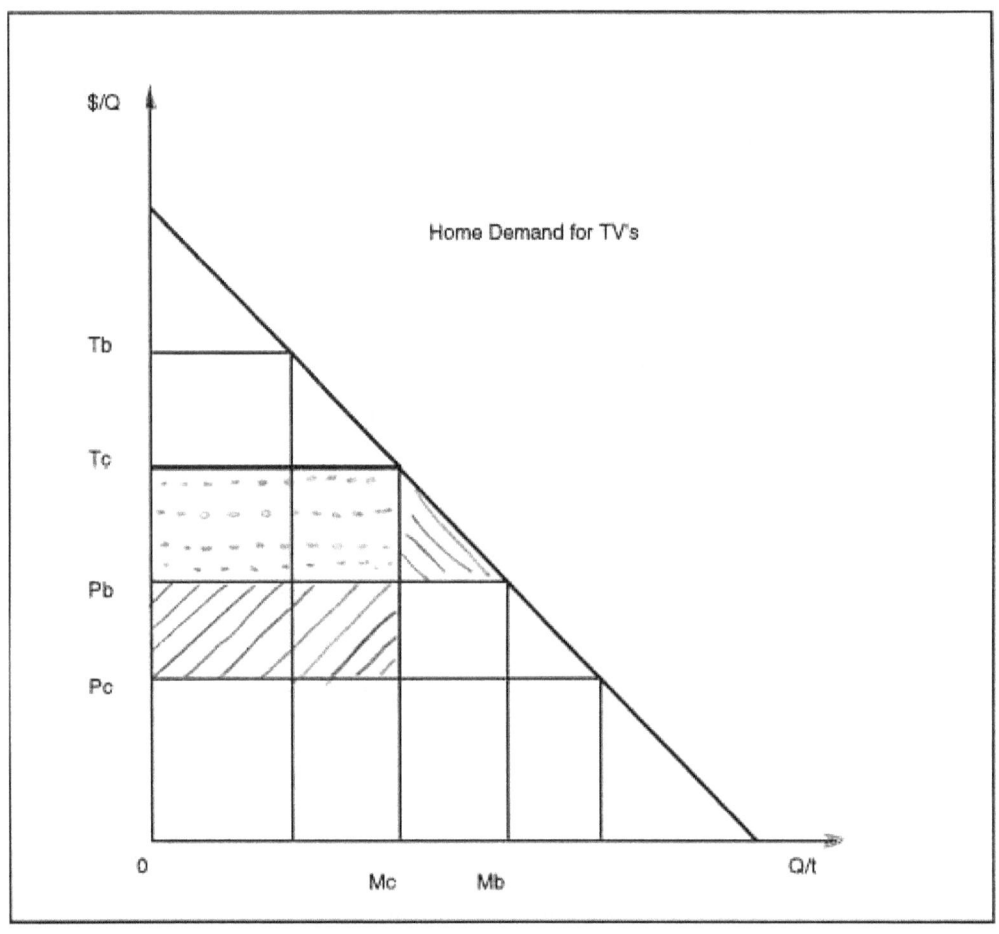

if no tariff: Pc < Pb
if tariff on B and C: Tc < Tb
if tariff only on C: Pb < Tc

"//////" = loss from tariff revenue that used to be in for the Government but now will go to inefficient country B (here the US).

"11\\\\" = welfare gain from lowering tariff (this is a simple Harberger triangle).

So trade diversion will lead to a net welfare loss if "///////" is larger than "\\\\\\".

What about the area ":::::"?

In fact, this area is neither a gain nor a loss for the Canadian economy: because while it is the loss of tariff revenue for the Government, it is a gain for the consumers (it is now part of the consumer surplus).
Remember, the consumer surplus is measured in $/t. It is a flow (NOT a stock!) like the GNP.

www.ingramcontent.com/pod-product-compliance
Lightning Source LLC
Chambersburg PA
CBHW080945170526
45158CB00008B/2383